South West Coast Yawl Rowing Association

– *A History*

Edited by Carol Gilbert

South West Coast Yawl Rowing Association

First Published in 2005
by
South West Coast Yawl Rowing Association
Fishers Cross
Castlefreke
Clonakilty
Co Cork
Ireland
© South West Coast Yawl Rowing Association 2005

British Library Cataloguing in Publication Data
A CIP catalogue record for this book is available from the British Library

ISBN 0-9550307-0-6

Typeset and Printed by Inspire Design and Print, Skibbereen, Co Cork
The authors acknowledge funding by The Heritage Council

SUPPORTED BY THE HERITAGE COUNCIL

LE CUIDIÚ AN CHOMHAIRLE OIDHREACHTA

SOUTH WEST COAST YAWL ROWING ASSOCIATION

Having been involved in rowing, in one way or another, all my life, I am particularly proud, as President of the South West Coast Yawl Rowing, to see this record of yawl rowing in West Cork come to its completion. Every endeavour has been made to source this information and to provide an accurate record of the beginning and setting up of the Association.

I wish it every success and thank everyone involved.

Pat Deasy
President
South West Coast Yawl Rowing Association

* * *

The following is a history of the coastal rowing clubs of West Cork, from Kilmacsimon in the east, to Bantry in the west, which today form the South West Coast Yawl Rowing Association.

The words and stories have been written by the men and women of West Cork themselves, the rowers, the coaches, the fundraisers, the committees and those who work behind the scenes.

Carol Gilbert
Editor
October 2004

ACKNOWLEDGEMENTS

The principal sources for this book are the men and women of West Cork's coastal communities and members of the South West Yawl Rowing Association, who have researched their clubs' minute books, put their memories down on paper, donated all the photographs used herein, and The Southern Star newspaper, Ilen Street, Skibbereen, by whose kind permission various excerpts have been reproduced.

The South West Coast Yawl Rowing Association gratefully acknowledge and wish to thank everyone involved in any way in the compilation of this book including, Bill Deasy, Pat and Ina Deasy, Donal Calnan, Anne Cochrane Townsend, Margaurite Deasy, John Duggan, Anthony and Rosarie Glanton, Julie Harrington, Ann Hawkins, Mary Hayes, John Keohane, JJ McCarthy, Carmel Mulcahy, Mick Murphy, Nick Norris, Michael O'Brien, Alex O'Donovan, Bernie O'Donovan, Billy O'Driscoll, Úna O'Mahony, Dr Mary O'Neill, Caroline Vickery, and everyone who has contributed in any way to its completion.

We thank Carol Gilbert for her assistance from the beginning of this project through to its completion.

We gratefully acknowledge the sponsorship from our advertisers.

We thank Nick Bendon and his staff at CH Marine for their ongoing support over the years.

We thank Liam O'Regan and the staff of *The Southern Star* for their coverage of events, facilitating researchers and for assistance with the research, and finally we thank Bill Deasy, who was concerned this information would be lost, whose idea it was to collate and record it for future generations, and for his and Nick Norris's endeavours in taking the project through to completion.

CONTENTS

THE ORIGINS OF COASTAL ROWING

The sport of Coastal Rowing can be traced as far back as the old cobblers and fishing boats used by fishermen of the mid-Nineteenth Century, and probably long before this. Coastal rowing is a sport that has been enjoyed around the coast of Ireland for many years. Rowing regattas have been part of the life and folklore of this island for a hundred years or more, but traditionally, boats used for racing were working fishing boats used on a daily basis to earn a living.

Crews of boats and cobblers are recorded as racing out to meet incoming schooners, with the winners receiving the valuable piloting contract, or being employed in the loading/unloading of the ship or securing cargo or catch for an agent. There was also the benefit of racing to the best fishing grounds where they could expect to take the best catch of fish, so coastal rowing began as a means of earning a living and of survival.

Races were rowed every Sunday, in one locality, with the fishermen from each village rowing against teams from neighbouring villages making use of the natural facilities of small harbours for the event. The weekly regatta would be rowed at a different venue and during their spare time and holidays, coastal crews raced for sport and for many rural areas, this sport was the only one available through geographical restrictions of coastal areas. Races were fiercely contested, as the prize was usually either a keg of porter, or a cash prize.

At a regatta in Schull in 1893, the 1st Prize was £1 and 2nd Prize was 10 shillings, a small fortune in those days. These regattas would have been a major event in the locality and would have been eagerly awaited by both young and old. There are records of the lobster boats of Heir Island and Roaringwater Bay taking part in many local regattas.

Rowing would be just one of the many events that would take place on regatta day. Other competitions could include sailing, the pig and pole, swimming races, step dancing, as well as a host of other events. In the early 1930's a number of Six Oar Gigs were built and raced at regattas all along the coast. Boat, crew and supporters would be transported all aboard a lorry. These boats were raced for a number of years, but the interest faded during the War.

Rowing made a comeback in the late 1950's and 1960's, when a number of gigs were built and raced at various venues along the coast, but interest waned again.

In the 1970's rowing clubs began to organise themselves and a number of people got together and formed an association in West Cork.

The popularity of the sport grew rapidly over the next few years, so much so that in the late 1980's the number of teams became too much to be accommodated in one harbour. It was at this point the decision was made to divide Cork County into two, with Kinsale, and those clubs to the east of Kinsale, forming the Coastal Rowing Federation and the clubs to the west of Kinsale forming the South West Coastal Rowing Association.

In the early days of coastal rowing the boats were used as workboats during the week and raced at weekends but, by the 1930's, clubs began to commission boats. Because they would all have been built by different boat builders, some were faster than others, with the result that often it was not the best crew that was winning, but the best boat. In addition, pleasure craft would be entered into the very popular competitions and regattas, which, during the summer, attracted huge attendances. At times, as many as nine different types of boat were competing in the one race.

In 1994 Rob Jacob, a boat designer based in Kinsale, was contracted by the Irish Coastal Rowing Federation Ltd. to design a 4-oar racing yawl in order to bring parity to the sport. All championship races must now be competed in the one design boat providing a level playing field for all competitors. Irish Coastal Rowing is a 32 County sport and in the first All Ireland, when the new one design boat was used, which was competed in Carnlough, Co Antrim in 2002, ten different clubs succeeded in taking All Ireland honours, thus proving the success of the one design boat.

The one design rowing yawl, is 24 ft long, with a dry hull weight of 130 kgs max, and is built of fibreglass.

The sport of coastal rowing is open to teams ranging from under 12's to veteran.

Competitors compete in Veteran Ladies, Under 16's, Under 16 Ladies, Under 18 Ladies, Pre Veteran Men, Junior Ladies, Under 12s, Intermediate, Veteran Mixed, Pre Veteran Ladies, Junior Men, Veteran Men, Under 18s, Senior Men, Senior Mixed, Under 21s, Under 14s and Under 14 Ladies. In All Ireland competitions where clubs compete for the coveted Club of the

Year Championship, additional classes are Open Classic Men, Open Classic Ladies, Out Riggers Men, and the Seine Boat Race.

There are physical differences between the boats used under ICRF and IARU regulations, necessary mainly because of the different environment used for the sport: open seas –vs- rivers or lakes. The rowing action is different, as sea rowing requires a completely different technique and a different training regime. Also with the modern day level of focus on safety, ICRF has its own set of rules and regulations, which include the wearing of life jackets at all times, safety boats in attendance and stewards.

Race lengths are different and all coastal rowing involves rowing within designated lanes of buoys and turning around a buoy at sea. Courses vary between short – 600m, middle – 1000m, long – 1750.

Original participants in the past were from working class communities, in particular from farming and fishing, and today many of the present day competitors are following the tradition of a sport steeped in their ancestry.

Coastal rowing has, over the years, succeeded in sustaining small rural communities through the use of natural local facilities and by encouraging team and community spirit by training and competing together. Participation is non-discriminatory, open to everyone, of all ages, and provides an opportunity to integrate within the sport, regardless of cultural, religious, political or physical differences.

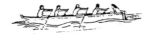

FOUNDING OF WEST CORK YAWL ROWING ASSOCIATION

Bill O'Driscoll was a founder member of the West Cork Yawl Rowing Association. His main interest was to get all the Regatta Committees in West Cork to carry out the same rules for their races and boats. At that time the yawls were more or less working boats. When the Association was formed they made a rule that any new boats built for racing could not be longer than 21 feet overall and 4 ft 6 inches beam. They could be carvel planked or clinker planked. They also arranged a West Cork Championship. They asked the Regatta Committees to put down a buoy for each boat in the race at the turning point. At that time, only one buoy was put at the turning point for all competing boats, which created numerous problems for the boats if they arrived at the buoy at the same time. There would be objections lodged with the committee when the race was finished which took a lot of skill to sort out.

This committee continued to work together for about six years, following which the membership increased and the rules were extended to establish County and All Ireland Championships. They also allowed the boats to be changed a little and encouraged fibreglass boats to be used in the racing.

The Irish Coastal Rowing Federation was formed in 1991 as a national organisation incorporating seven rowing associations, representing forty-five clubs. During the 1995 All Ireland, the Irish Coastal Rowing Federation banner, newly designed in green, white and gold, featuring the Federation's emblem of crossed oars was unveiled and flown for the first time.

Today all the boats in West Cork are of the same design and were designed by Rob Jacob, a Kinsale-based yacht designer, who took the yawl design and produced a light, fast racing boat. At present the South West Yawl Rowing Association is one of the strongest rowing associations in the country.

The clubs of the South West Coastal Yawl Rowing Association include, Ardfield/Rathbarry, Bantry, Castletownshend, Courtmacsherry, Kilmacabea, Kilmacsimon, Myross, Ring, Rosscarbery, Schull and Sherkin Island, and over the last number of years, the clubs from the South West have taken top honours at the All Ireland Championships.

The following is their story.

Ardfield – Rathbarry Rowing Club

Ardfield-Rathbarry Rowing Club was formed in January 1985. The Club was formed with the main intention of reviving the old tradition of rowing which had existed in the Parish, up to fifty years before, to promote the sport of rowing for all age groups, especially the youth, and to improve the facilities of one of the parish's biggest natural assets, Kilkern Lake.

The Club's first boat, "The Galley Flash", bought from Billy O'Driscoll of Baltimore, was blessed at Rathbarry Church and launched at Kilkern Lake on February 2nd, 1985.

In the first year of competition the Club won three South West Coast Championships and went from strength to strength over the next few years.

In 1986 a song was composed by the Club called, "The Boys of the Galley Flash" and was frequently sung by Club members and supporters.

During the winter of 1985/86, the Club organised swimming lessons at Dunmanway Swimming Pool and these lessons were very well attended as new members were joining the Club.

The Club built their boathouse at Kilkern Lake in 1987 and much fundraising was organised for this project because the cost of the building came to approximately £2,500.

Ardfield-Rathbarry Rowing Club enjoyed successful years in the late 1980's at South West and All-Ireland Championship level. The Club still hold the All-Ireland Champions at both Ladies' and Gents' 2-Oar races as these are no longer part of the All-Ireland programme. Vet Ladies winners in Kilmacsimon in July 1984 were Kathleen Harrington, Mary Deasy, Mary McSweeney and Eileen Whelton. Winners of the 2-oar ladies' boat race at Baltimore Regatta in 1986 were Anita Murphy, Liz Fagan and cox Noel Fitzpatrick. Winners at Kilmacsimon Regatta August 1986, were, Ladies' 4-oars, Liz Fagan, Martina O'Sullivan, Maura Lyne, Anita Murray and cox Noel Fitzpatrick. Winners of the Snr Men's 4-oars, Jim Fitzpatrick, Donal O'Donovan, Michael Feen, Denis Murray, and Noel Fitzpatrick again the cox.

Michael Harrington (cox), Hazel Hurley, Kate O'Brien, Sandra Hayes, Tracy Lombard. U14 Ladies All Ireland winners 2000 in Schull.

Tracy Lombard, Aisling Feen, Sandra Hayes, Hazel Hurley, U16 Ladies 2004, Union Hall Regatta.

Niamh Tobin, Lisa Hayes, Aine Hayes, Laura Connolly. U12 S.W.C.Y.R.A. Championship Winners and All Ireland Winners 2004.

In the early 1990's a team from East Cork joined the Association and the Championships were dominated by Cobh with Ardfield-Rathbarry/The Galley coming second. Results of the Ardfield-Rathbarry Regatta in 1993, were, U12, 1. Courtmacsherry, 2. Kilmacsimon, 3. Clon. U14, 1. Clon., 2 Courtmac., 3. Galley Flash. Vet-Men, 1. Kilmacsimon, 2. Galley Flash, 3. Ring. Vet Ladies, 1. Galley Flash, 2. Kilmacsimon. U16, 1. Ring, 2. Courtmac, 2. Kilmacsimon. Mixed, 1. Ring, 2. Courtmac., 3. Kilmacsimon. Junior Men, 1. Kilmacsimon, 2. Ring, 3. Clon. Snr Ladies, 1. Clon, 2. Ring, 3. Courtmac. Snr Men, 1. Kilmacsimon, 2. Clon., 3. Courtmacsherry.

In 1994 a new boat was purchased by the Club which again brought success at Championship, County and All-Ireland level and the Club has enjoyed success at all age levels from U-12's up to Veterans. The Galley Flash ladies' team, who were winners at the Kilmacsimon Regatta in 1994, were Bernadette O'Donovan, Annette Harte, Una O'Mahony, Ann Crowley, and cox James Fitzpatrick.

The U14 Ladies were all Ireland Champions in Schull 2001 and U18 Men won the AIB All Ireland Championship in Carnlough 2002. Fundraising and grants enabled the club to purchase a new One Design Boat. In the new "Galley Flash III" the U18's came second in the 2003 All Ireland in Kerry and the U12's came 3rd.

Whitegate Rowing Club hosted the 2004 All Ireland in August and the "Galley Flash III" brought home firsts for the U12's, U14's and Under 14 Ladies' teams. Pre-Vet Ladies came 2nd, U18's 2nd and U21's 3rd, making Ardfield-Rathbarry Rowing Club runner up for Club of the Year.

Over the years, rowing has brought great pleasure and enjoyment to both young and old of the parish. We hope to continue this enjoyment for many years to come and hope that the words of "The Boys of the Galley Flash" will continue to be heard.

The Boys of The Galley Flash

In the morning, as light is dawning
I see young men, set their craft upon the sea
They are training for the day when
They'll be bringing home the cup for all to see

Chorus:
We'll make music on the water
We'll beat rhythm with the swinging of the oar
Men are heaving, crowds are cheering
When the boys of the Galley Flash come rowing

home

Oh the sound of water lapping
Making music echoes all around the shore
They tell loved ones with their singing
Tales of sorrow they have passed forever more

Chorus

Some men take to drinking whiskey
Some men follow the bowling and the score
But the Galley crew are happy
When they're on the wave and heaving fast for
home

Chorus

Now it's time for jubilation and debating
On the days of events since past
In the cup of celebration are the dreams
For the future and the echoes of the past

Chorus

© **Galley Flash Rowing Club, Castlefreke**

Bantry Rowing Club

Boat racing has gone on in Bantry Bay for many years. Seine boats from Whiddy, Bere Island, Gearhies, Bantry and Adrigole were involved in many famous tussles. The traditional West Cork gig, 40 ft long and canvassed fore and aft put in its appearance before the first War. This gig was used in Bantry Bay and Kenmare Bay and in the early days, Bere Island and Whiddy Island were the main protagonists with the famous Casey brothers of Sneem achieving glory in the late 1930's.

Regattas took place in Bantry, Castletownbere and Bere Island, with gig racing and rowing races for all manner of other rowing boats; two, four and six oar boats all featured.

Bantry Rowing Club was founded in 1963. Tom Mullins and John Hunt borrowed a gig from Whiddy Island and got a crew together, coxed by Ginger Downey of Whiddy.

This crew did quite well and next year had a boat built by Dennis (Kilderry) Keohane of Ballylickey. A number of successful years followed in Senior and Junior rowing.

In the early 1970's, Ladies' and Under Age rowing took off and the Club

Bantry, Wales and N. Ireland long-boats.

Bantry longboat crew 2003.

began to do well in these disciplines. Senior rowing at this time went downhill and did not ressurrect until the mid-seventies and early eighties.

At this stage the club joined the Irish Amateur Rowing Union and became involved in sliding seat rowing at a National level.

Bantry crews won National titles with Junior Ladies' Double scull in 1998 and National Sprint titles with Ladies' Double, Ladies' Novice eights and Men's Novice eights and fours.

In 1998 the Club quad and double represented Ireland at the home International in Scotland, and again, in 1999, Bantry scullers represented

John Hunt, Majella O'Mahony and Dr Matt Murphy (October 2004).

Ireland in the European Junior Cup.

In 1988, the Club became involved in the Atlantic Challenge which races in traditional wooden longboats. This involves taking part in International competitions every two years. The Bantry crew, representing Ireland, won the Atlantic Challenge in Canada in 1994, in France in 2000 and in Maine USA in 2002.

In 2000 the Club decided to get involved in yawl boat racing and purchased an ancient relic from Schull. The Club are extremely grateful to Courtmacsherry for the loan of a boat, which enabled Bantry to take part in its first regatta season in 2001. Jnr Men were 2nd and U-16 Ladies 3rd in the All Ireland held in Schull in 2001. A one design boat was ordered and the rowers enjoyed a good season winning the Under 21's and Snr Men's at the All Ireland held in Carlough, Co Antrim, in 2002. In 2003 the Club had a good year, winning at a number of regattas. The Senior Men won at some regattas, the Junior Ladies were 2nd or 3rd, and U-16 Men were second most of the year. At the 2003 All Ireland, held in Cromane, Co Kerry, the Snr Men won, U-16 Men won, and Junior Ladies just missed out on a medal by coming 4th. In 2004 at the All Ireland in East Cork, Bantry Senior Men took gold.

Bantry's one design boat is called "Smoke 'n' Mirrors" and the club lease a timber boat from Ring.

Following on from their 2004 All Ireland win, the Bantry Snr Men's team, Liam Young, Luke O'Donovan, Merlin Tanner, Michael Spillane and cox,

Presentation to teams competing in World Coastal Rowing Challenge 2004. Bill Deasy, Dr Matt Murphy, Declan Crowley, Catriona Lane, John O'Leary and Alex O'Donovan.

Liam Young, Luke O'Donovan, Merlin Tanner, Michael Spillane and cox Majella O'Mahony, flying the flag for Ireland at La Grande Motte, Montpellier, France, October 2004.

Majella O'Mahony, were invited by the Irish Coastal Rowing Federation to represent Ireland, at the World Coastal Rowing Challenge, held at La Grande Motte, Montpellier, France, on 17th October 2004. The crew travelled out with a large number of supporters, and took to the waters in a field of 50-plus boats, comprising singles, doubles and quads, with half a dozen six oar boats competing for good measure. The Bantry team came in a very respectable fifth, an exceptional result considering the French boats were longer, narrower, and sliders and the race was only the third time the crew had sat in this type of boat, so a great achievement all round.

2004 officers of the club are, President: Alex O'Donovan, Chair: Geraldine Young, Captain: Liam Young, Secretary: Matt Murphy. The Atlantic Challenge has a website at www.atlanticchallenge.org

Castletownshend Rowing Club

There has been a much longer history of championship regattas in Castletownshend than there has been of a rowing club. During a Regatta meeting in Lil McCarthy's Bar in March 1996, a teenager from the village approached the Chairman of the Regatta Committee and requested that the Regatta Committee get a rowing boat for the village. He was told to go and get a list of people who would be interested in rowing and came back with more than 20 names on the list. Joe Hawkins, as chairman of the Regatta Committee, approached the South West Yawl Rowing committee with a view to hiring or buying a suitable boat and he was informed that Courtmacsherry had a boat for sale.

Joe Hawkins and Dick Kelly borrowed a boat, one set of oars and a trailer from Courtmacsherry, the old Galley Flash/Courtmacsherry yawl having been built by Billy O'Driscoll of Baltimore.

A Rowing Club committee was founded following a meeting called in the GAA pavilion and Breda O'Driscoll was elected as chairper-

Peter Magnier presenting clothing and equipment to Joe Hawkins, PRO, Irish Coastal Rowing Federation, prior to the Castletownshend Snr Ladies and Bantry Snr Men's teams competing in the World Rowing Challenge in Montpellier, France, October 2004. Peter and his late wife, Jane, have been great benefactors to the Castletownshend Rowing Club.

Anne Cochrane-Townshend, Margaret Cahalane, Betsy Didderiens, Tess Cahalane and Declan Crowley. Winners of the Vet Ladies All Ireland in Schull 2001.

son of the first committee, and so children began rowing every evening at the main pier. Whilst there was great enjoyment for all ages, the biggest problem proved to be the funds necessary to keep the rowing club functioning. Mr Peter Magnier, who has a home in the village, saw the enjoyment the children and young people were having and kindly donated the money to buy lifejackets and a boat and formally got the club up and running. This boat was called the "Naoimh Barrachain". So began Castletownshend Rowing Club's involvement in regattas, and although initially not very successful, they did not always come last.

Other clubs in the South West Yawl Rowing Association were in the process of buying new boats and the decision was taken, that if Castletownshend were to succeed, they had to purchase a more up to date boat. Following a meeting held in 1998 a door to door collection around the Parish for funds raised part of the money needed and by the time a number of fundraising events were held there was enough money to put in an order for a new boat. Castletownshend Rowing Cub now had a very strong committee and Ray O'Callaghan, Kinsale, was commissioned to build the new boat which was called "The Hurricane".

With the new boat, and a new set of donated oars, the club started to improve its rankings and began to grow from strength to strength attracting new members. Their first All Ireland medal was in Kinsale in 1998, when they achieved 1 bronze and 3 silver medals. As they began to climb the rankings in local regattas, in 1999 in Glandore, Castletownshend won their first County Title with their Senior Ladies' team taking gold. Their first All Ireland title was achieved the same year with the Senior Ladies' team taking gold in Ringsend, Dublin. In 2000 they won some championships and in the County Championships in Union Hall won 3 gold, 5 silver and 5 bronze medals, earning the title of Club of the Day. In the All Ireland which was held in Wexford in 2000, Castletownshend won 3 gold and 2 bronze medals, growing stronger and gaining new members. In 2001 they again won some championships and in the All Ireland in Schull, won 6 gold and 4 bronze medals.

2002 saw one of the biggest changes in rowing with the introduction of the one-design rowing yawl for County and All Ireland rowing regattas. This boat was commissioned and introduced by the Irish Coastal Rowing Federation, enabling each team to compete from a level playing field, as prior to the introduction of the one-design yawl, up to nine different boats could compete in the same race.

The new boat was fibreglass, replacing the traditional wooden rowing boat, thus changing the course of rowing in West Cork and all over Ireland. Jane and Peter Magnier kindly sponsored the new boat and Castletownshend took delivery of the one-design yawl in 2002.

The Club won many championships in 2002 and their achievements were crowned during the 2002 AIB All Ireland Coastal Rowing Championships which were held in Carnlough, Co Antrim. Castletownshend began their long journey home heavily laden with 4 gold and 4 silver medals and the coveted AIB Club of the Year trophy.

The Club was fortunate to receive a major boost in 2002 from Mrs Margaret Warren, when she donated the O'Mahony Boathouse on the Western Pier to the Club for the use of the community, a very generous gift everyone will be eternally grateful for. Major refurbishments took place with toilets, showers and gym facilities being installed. This extended the training regime for the members and the official opening of the new club house took place in June 2003, Mrs Margaret Warren cutting the red ribbon.

2003 was again a bumper year for the Club, winning 7 Championship titles, and at the AIB All Ireland Championships in Cromane, Co Kerry taking 8 gold, 3 silver and 2 bronze medals and the AIB Club of the Day award for the second year in a row.

In August 2004, with county championship titles again under the belt, they travelled to Whitegate, East Cork, with high hopes of achieving the

Castletownshend PreVet Men, Colm Cahalane, Donal O'Mahony, MC O'Mahony, Martin Cahalane and cox Padraig Murphy.

Sheer concentration from the 2003 U18's Shane Crowley, Damien O'Neill, Ian Hurley, Jamie O'Driscoll and Declan Crowley.

The plaque commemorating her late husband Bayard.

Mrs Margaret "Tommy" Warren cuts the red ribbon at the official opening of the Boathouse.

Official opening of Boathouse in 2002.

Shane Crowley, Catriona Lane, Eileen Whooley, Lisa Cahalane, Aisling O'Neill, Snr Ladies 2003, in the new one design yawl to left Dick Kelly to right Joe Brien.

At the AIB Bank Presentation as Club of the Year, 2004: Pat McCarthy, Seamus Walsh, Padraig Murphy, Paddy Hurley and Donal O'Mahony.

Snr Ladies in La Grande Motte: Eileen Whooley, Lisa Cahalane, Declan Crowley, Catriona Lane and Mary McCarthy.

triple. They came home with 8 gold, 4 silver and 1 bronze medal, making them AIB All Ireland Club of the Day for the third consecutive year.

Their success was tinged with sadness, because their great benefactor and staunch supporter, Mrs Margaret "Tommy" Warren, passed away around the time they achieved the triple. Their other great benefactor, Jane Magnier, had died earlier that month.

The Club's winning Senior Ladies' team at the AIB All Ireland were invited by the Irish Coastal Rowing Federation, to compete in the World Coastal Rowing Challenge in Montpellier, France, on 17th October 2004. The team were extremely successful, securing second place for Ireland, in a field of 45, and bringing home silver to the village.

Castletownshend Rowing Club's successes have been remarkable in the few years since the club was founded. This is due in no small measure to the dedication and support of rowers, members and the large team working behind the scenes.

Courtmacsherry Rowing Club

Although Courtmacsherry Rowing Club, as it exists at the moment, began in 1991, the history of rowing locally goes back to the early 1900's when a number of clubs existed. Courtmacsherry has a long history of competitive rowing and many people remember the famous teams of old taking their boats and crews throughout West Cork. Even during the war years, when there were severe restrictions and fuel was rationed, John O'Driscoll, Broad Strand, often used his lorry to carry the clinker built boat (Harts' boat from Clonakilty) with the supporters crammed underneath to Rosscarbery and further afield. I am told that John was a past master at taking short cuts over hill and dale to avoid the garda check points, which were a common feature during the Emergency.

The local schoolmaster, John Sheehy, used to travel behind the cab with the rest of the excited brigade. The motto was, "get under the boat if it starts raining." Since the truck had to take a circuitous route, the crew often cycled to regattas with their favourite oar strapped to the cross bar of the bike. "Favourite" here meant that the owner had to use the plane and spoke shave to lighten the oar to a precision implement. If one had the misfortune to beat a local crew in their home port, the shortest and fastest way home would be the most favoured option.

In the 1930's the famous Fr Sheehy commissioned the building of two purpose built racing boats in the Industrial School in Baltimore and on August Monday, the Courtmacsherry Lifeboat was used to tow the two boats to Kinsale for the day's racing. These were the first purpose built racing craft, as up to then the boats used were working boats and some were used for salmon fishing in the local estuary. On regatta day in Courtmac', boats with names like, "Star of the Sea", "Half Heir", "Kilty Lass", would be familiar sites at the pier head.

Like many of the great oarsmen of the past, many of their descendants are stepping on board to take up the challenge and again history is repeating itself. Courtmac' has two boats and John O'Driscoll's grandsons are

Courtmac in training alongside the Courtmacsherry Lifeboat.

involved in both rowing and transporting the craft. Crew members are now taking up rowing positions where their fathers and grandfathers sat before them. From the mid-60's Courtmacsherry Regatta programme had mainly concentrated on athletics and swimming events with smaller boat races. In 1981 the regatta committee secured a number of four-oar boat crews, and teams from Baltimore, Glandore and Clonakilty competed in the Regatta.

The Southern Star of 22nd August 1981 says, "Yes indeed the crews from these three places (Baltimore, Glandore and Clonakilty) brought back a touch of the old atmosphere to Courtmacsherry Regatta. They also brought a touch of colour and variety with four crews in all, including a mixed crew and all ladies crew."

"In the Junior men's there were four boats, but it was really a race between Baltimore's "Rising Sun" and Glandore's "Cu-na-Mara", with the latter crew of, Dan Donoghue, Nicky Bendon, Murt O'Sullivan and Pat Hayes, just getting the verdict by about two lengths. In this race also Glandore's Brown Boat and "The Kilty Lass" from Clonakilty, put in a commendable performance. "The Kilty Lass" is a namesake of another famous rowing boat of the not too distant past."

"In the ladies' race, the Glandore crew of Ann Kelleher, Frances O'Regan, Ann McCarthy and Frances Hayes were well in command all through and won by a good distance."

"However it was the clash of the senior crews of Baltimore and Glandore which provided the most exciting spectacle. With both crews rounding their buoys near the Gravelly Point simultaneously, everybody was set for a real thriller and they weren't disappointed because as both boats battled up the channel against the dropping tide, they were locked together in what has been described as the greatest boat race ever seen at a regatta in Courtmacsherry. Eventually it was the Glandore crew, powered by the McCarthy brothers of Glandore Castle, who edged in front to win by less than half a length. Both crews earned great applause from the huge crowd on that quayside. The members of the Glandore crew were, Pat McCarthy (stroke), Joe Hamilton, Charlie McCarthy and Tim O'Regan with Michael O'Regan acting as cox for the three winning crews. All these races were held under the auspices of the South West Cork Yawl Rowing Federation."

Courtmacsherry Regatta Day of June 1991 attracted huge crowds to the village. Clonakilty Rowing Club organised a rowing event in aid of the local lifeboat. A number of crews from other clubs took part, rowing the Clon racing boat from Glandore to Courtmacsherry, and four women took the boat on its final stretch into Courtmacsherry pier, where they were escorted from the outer harbour by the lifeboat. On 1st December 1991, a meeting was held at Courtmacsherry Community Hall to discuss the possibility of reviving rowing in the village. After a long discussion among the large attendance, it was decided to form a club and the following officers were elected, Chairman: Danny Holland, Secretary: Martin McCarthy, Treasurer: John Colgan. It was agreed to go ahead and raise funds to purchase a boat.

The following week the officers of the club, along with John Young and Diarmuid O'Mahoney went collecting locally and in one night had the £1,200 necessary collected. They then went ahead and purchased the "June Rose" from Ring Rowing Club, which was renamed "Challenger" and launched on Whit weekend 1992. The Club was very successful in its first year with up to 60 members, mainly under the age of 16. Under the guidance of coach, Martin McCarthy, these teenagers were the foundation on which future success was built. The Courtmac U16 crew had a successful outing at the Castletownshend Regatta, July 1992, with Brian Whelton, John O'Connor, Norman Fleming and Daniel Whelton crossing the line first.

In 1993, it was decided to build a new boat for a sport that was becoming increasingly popular, both locally and nationally. This boat, was the first boat of this design to be built for racing in West Cork. "The Argideen" was launched mid season in 1993, and this led to a record number of All Ireland medals the following year in Baltimore with the U-18's consisting of Brian Whelton, Declan McCarthy, John O'Connor, Daniel Whelton and cox Norman Fleming, bringing home the Club's first All-Ireland gold medal. U-12's, Jnr Ladies and Intermediate Men's also brought home All-Ireland medals. The Club has continued to bring home All-Ireland medals on seven occasions, out of the following eight years.

With rowing boats being standardised for the first time, a new one-design fibreglass boat is being introduced for All-Ireland racing. Courtmacsherry Rowing Club, who have again led the way by placing the first order for one of these boats, look forward to a successful future in yawl rowing.

Remember "mens sana in corpora sano" or a healthy mind in a healthy body.

Courtmac' Regatta

Once again tis August and the shorting of the day brings a tinge of sweet nostalgia for the summer past away, and like corn fields in the setting sun a kind of golden glow, surrounds the happy memories of summers long ago.

As simple country children, the summer holidays were spent in blissful freedom in those carefree sunny days. June, July, the time would fly till August came the way, to bring the high point of our lives, Courtmac' Regatta day.

For weeks before we'd count the days as August did draw near we hoped the weather would hold out with sunshine bright and clear, and when it did our hearts would sing as passing by Lislee we'd dream of what the day might bring in Courtmac by the sea.

As we cycled down around the lodge the sound of a pipe band came through the trees upon the breeze as if from fairy land, our hearts would race as we would face the bright and teaming street with bunting gay along the way and the sea and boats beneath.

How splendid looked those stately yachts upon the water blue, the lifeboat decked with splenden adding colour to the view, the puttering of outboards lent excitement to the scene, as a score or more of pleasure boats moved up and down between. The music of the bagpipes and the hawkers' cheerful cry, bananas, pears or apples 2 for three pence come and buy, the steam train at the station filled with passengers from Cork gave Courtmacsherry promenade the bustle of New York. Donkey, carts and pony traps and people on shanks mare the gentry in their motor cars would all assemble there.

Some would come by bicycle and more would come by sea

*from Seven Heads, Travara or from far Dunworley. The
sailing race the four oar gig out and round the buoy
Colebawn, Travara, Seven Heads excitement would run high
to a mighty roar from the crowded shore each crew would
sweat and strain with hearts of oak and sturdy strokes the
finish line to gain.*

*The pubs would do a roaring trade as many a man did
throat gave vent to pints of porter after pulling in a boat.
And as the gaul from Butlerstown was over heard to say "a
man would need two bellies to do justice to the day".*

*The road races the pig and pole the mighty pillow fight the
duck chase the sculling race with fire works for the night,
romance would often blossom at the dance in Hollands' Hall,
where Johnny Carty's music would re echo around the wall.*

*Denshy and ninety, Denis Murphy's starting gun, Billy
Murphy and the pillow fight would all add to the fun, a ram-
ble to the terrace to have tea in Walls café, would all
increase the magic of Courtmac Regatta Day.*

*The fancy dress would make us laugh and time would slip
away till sunset's lengthening shadows marked the closing of
the day. And high above the harbour, shun the mellow
autumn moon, as home we'd creep reluctant for to leave the
fun so soon.*

*Once again tis August and the lengthening of the night
reminds me of my lengthening years and time's remorseful
flight, my life may grow towards autumn but when I'm old
and grey I'll treasure happy memories of Courtmac Regatta
Day.*

by Michael O'Brien

Kilmacabea Rowing Club

Kilmacabea Rowing Club was reformed in 2002 after a lapse of 10 years. The club was initially founded in 1982 when four people, Tom Hayes, Pat Hayes, James Shanahan and Michael Scully, went to Oughterard in Co Galway to get a rowing boat built. The boat, which cost IR £1,200 was brought back to Glandore, named the "Cois Uisce" and the Club was successful, winning many championships and Club of the Year for three years in a row, 1982, 1983 and 984.

A large number of young people emigrated for employment in 1985, causing the club to fold, but in 1986 a group of people got together to set up the club again and a house-to-house collection took place to raise funds. Together with some local sponsorship, a new boat was purchased called the "St Fachtna" which was built in Reengaroga by Fachtna O'Sullivan. With this boat, the Club won Mixed, U12, U16 and Senior Ladies Championships, the U12 All Ireland title and Junior Ladies' team took second place in 1991.

Due to changes in Association rules, clubs were required to get bigger and better boats, and as Kilmacabea Rowing Club did not have sufficient funds, unfortunately the Club once again folded.

In February 2002, a group of six people got together in the Morris Arms, Connonagh, and decided to get the Club back on the water again. A large number of people attended a meeting, organised for the end of February, during which officers were elected and the hard work started again. In early May 2002, the "St Fachtna" was pulled out of storage and training commenced.

Castletownshend was the Club's first regatta, with around eight crews taking part, and although there were no wins on the day, the Club got a great welcome back to shore. In July 2002 the Club bought the "May Queen" from Kilmacsimon Rowing Club and this boat allowed the Club to take part in regattas on a better level with the other clubs.

At the AGM in December 2002 and after a great deal of deliberation, it was decided to buy the new one-design boat. An order was placed that month and with help from the Club's supporters, a deposit raised and paid.

Kilmacabea U-16 Ladies Jenny Quirke, Niamh O'Riordan, Ann-Marie O'Sullivan, Angela Collins and cox, Mary Hayes, Castletownshend Regatta 2004.

The new boat, "The Rocket" was blessed in Glandore on 29th June 2003 and the Club went from strength to strength for the rest of the season, winning the U16 Ladies and U12 Championships, with the Pre-Vet Ladies getting a third.

Club supporters headed off on August 22nd 2003 to Cromane, Co Kerry, for the AIB All-Ireland Rowing Regatta. All crews qualified for finals on the Sunday and the U16 Ladies' crew, Jenny Quirke, Niamh O'Riordan, Ann-Marie O'Sullivan, Angela Collins and cox Mary Hayes, won the first gold medal for the Club. Then the U12 crew of Sean O'Regan, Liam Cronin, Nicola O'Sullivan, Aoife O'Riordan and cox, Karl McCarthy, brought the second gold medal home.

Kilmacabea Rowing Club had a successful season in 2004 gaining five 2nds and four 3rds in the South West Championships. They achieved a gold medal at the AIB All Ireland in East Cork, their Mixed Vet team coming in first and a silver in the Intermediate Men's race. Further success was to come in the annual charity row from Cobh in Cork Harbour on September 5th 2004. Each competing club has to raise substantial entrance money, with the prize being a new one design yawl. Only two West Cork teams competed this year, Kilmacabea and Myross and for the first time the prize of a new boat went to West Cork and Kilmacabea.

With two boats, Kilmacabea looks forward to a successful and happy future.

Kilmacabea and Schull.

Kilmacabea Under 12's at Castletownshend Regatta 2002.

Under 16 Ladies' crew at Cromane, Co Kerry for the AIB All Ireland, 2003, Jenny Quirke, Niamh O'Riordan, Ann-Marie O'Sullivan, Angela Collins and cox, Mary Hayes.

Cox Mary O'Sullivan with the 2004 U12's Ciara Twomey, Sean O'Regan, John O'Sullivan and Joseph Collins.

Kilmacsimon Swimming and Rowing Club

Kilmacsimon Quay is located on the western side of the Bandon Estuary between Innishannon and Kinsale. It has a long seafaring and fishing tradition and the local people, especially the members of Kilmacsimon Swimming & Rowing Club, are justifiably proud of it. Ships carrying coal, fertilizer and other commodities used to dock at the quay for over one hundred years. Now there is a boat sales business in the quay, which is run by Paul Kingston, and fishermen like, Neilus Keohane and Mick Murphy, who continue to fish by the draft method, are modern day reminders of the quay's heritage.

There has always been a great fishing tradition at Kilmacsimon Quay. At one time there were six yawls fishing out of the quay. The Keohane's and the Keogh's owned two boats, with the Murphy's and Sweeney's owning one boat a piece. Every year during the carnivals at Kilmacsimon and Ballinadee a race was organised between the fishermen. These were straight races, approximately 2 miles in distance, usually from Collier's Quay to Kilmacsimon or the Corta to Ballinadee.

The boats used were the working yawls used for fishing every other day. There was always great excitement at this event especially as there was little else going on in the area at the time. One of the most famous boats around at the time, was called the "Glue Pot". She was owned by the Murphy's and later on the Keohane's and in all her races against the fishermen of Ballinadee she was never beaten. Her reputation became so great that on one occasion the fishermen swapped boats for the race with the Ballinadee men lining up in the much coveted boat. The outcome was a win for Ballinadee!

During the 1970's swimming was very popular off Kilmacsimon quay. Many learned to swim there, using a rope tied around their chest with their instructor keeping tension on the rope at the quay side. It was not unusual for the learner's cry of "pull in the rope" to be answered with "What? More rope is it!" Many swam regularly from Kilmacsimon to Gillman's Quay (known locally as "the Store") and on to Shippool Castle. On one occasion, J.J. McCarthy and Pat O' Neill swam from Kilmacsimon to Kinsale, a distance of some 8 miles.

Kilmacsimon Swimming Club was founded in 1980 and J.J. McCarthy, Pat O' Neill, Finbarr Deasy and Collette Keohane were the founder members. Lessons and instructors were organised for beginners, improvers and advanced swimmers. Life saving skills were also taught to club members, through the Irish Water Safety Association, and once qualified they in turn taught new members. This took place during the winter months and buses were organised to collect swimmers from the surrounding areas of Bandon, Ballinspittle, Ballinadee, Innishannon as well as the Kilmacsimon area itself. Initially these lessons were held at Dunmanway swimming pool but, as the numbers increased, an extra night each week was organised and the larger pool of Churchfield in Cork City was booked. Here life saving was taught through the Royal Life Saving Society and members also had the opportunity to go for the Bronze Medallion. It was not unusual to have over one hundred swimmers on any one night. A swimming gala was always organised for the last night of the season with great excitement and plenty of competition assured. Though the location of the swimming pools has varied over the years, the swimming lessons organised by the club are as popular and strongly subscribed today, and this activity is still pursued by the club.

Having proven their ability in swimming events, as well as the pillow fight, greasy pole and duck chase at regattas throughout West Cork, it was next decided to participate in rowing. 1984 saw the local people of Kilmacsimon compete in rowing events in West Cork for the first time. A boat was purchased for the sum of £1,000 with the aid of a bank loan from the AIB in Bandon and the name of the club was changed to Kilmacsimon Swimming & Rowing Club. This boat was built by Fachna O' Sullivan and was originally made for Long Island Rowing Club near Reengaroga. Long Island condemned her, however after only one race, and she was left idle in a loft for a year before being purchased by Kilmacsimon Swimming & Rowing Club. This was to prove a terrific buy as, after some initial reservations, (one crew member reportedly called it "a gauls game" during his first try!) Kilmacsimon's men's team, on their first year out, took the title of Senior South West Yawl Rowing Champions from the "Rising Sun", the then champions. The crew comprised of Mick Murphy, J.J. McCarthy, Eddie O'Neill, Pat O'Neill, sub Jerry Murphy and cox Patrick Morgan. The two-oar ladies' crew of Mary Kiely and Deirdre Keohane, not to be outdone by the men won the Two-Oar Ladies' South West Yawl Rowing Championship. These heroic

Kilmacsimon August 1955, Mick McCarthy, Philip Murphy, Dermot Murray, Denis Murphy, Dan Keogh.

1984 Kilmacsimon SW Senior 2-oar Ladies' Championships, Mary Kiely and Deirdre Keohane.

Kilmacsimon SW Senior Championships (Sherkin Island), cox, Patrick Morgan, Mick Murphy, JJ McCarthy, Eddie O'Neill and Pat O'Neill.

1985 Kilmacsimon SW Junior Champions, Clive Ross, Den Murphy, Patrick Morgan, cox, Jerrry Murphy, Taigh O'Regan (RIP).

Helen McCarthy, Carmel Mulcahy, Catherine Bernard, Sheila Crehan, (cox) Jeremy Keily. Pre-Vet Lds.

victories after such a short time led to great local interest in the club.

Also in this year a challenge was organised by Des Buggy, R.I.P., of Sherkin Island, between the South West Senior Champions, Kilmacsimon and the Dublin Senior Champions, Dalkey. The race was held at Sherkin Island with the Dublin crew competing in one of the Cork boats. Kilmacsimon were victorious on the day, winning the race by a clear six lengths. The crew from Dalkey, not to be outdone however, the following year invited the South West Senior Champions, who were again Kilmacsimon, to Dublin for a return leg. This time however, Kilmacsimon had to row in one of the Dublin boats! Although confident of their ability the different boat as well as the atrocious conditions proved too much for the Kilmacsimon crew and they were well beaten on the day. These challenges, which had never previously been contemplated, led to greater challenges being organised between the different rowing traditions around the country, resulting in the creation of the annual All-Ireland Rowing Championship itself.

The senior members of the club, especially J.J. McCrthy and Mary Kiely, devoted much of their time over the following years to train the new members who took up the sport.

The saddest day in the club's history was on the 12th of August 1995. Taigh O' Regan of Clohane, Kilmacsimon, died tragically whilst swimming in Kilmacsimon. He had been involved with the club since its foundation and had participated with several championship winning crews. May he rest in peace.

Today, members of Kilmacsimon Swimming & Rowing Club are proud of the fact they are involved with the longest continuously competing yawl rowing club in the South West. Since 1984 the club has competed in the South West Yawl Rowing Championship every year without fail, as well as the annual All-Ireland Rowing Championship (since its inauguration). Since its formation, Kilmacsimon have had no less than 5 boats. The first boat was simply called "Kilmacsimon" and the subsequent boats were "Rock Castle Pride", "The May Queen", "Naomh Brendan" and "Quay Breeze". "Rock Castle Pride" was designed and built by Jack Mons of Oughterard, Co.Galway in 1990 for £1,600. The "May Queen" was designed by Ron Holland, a world famous yacht designer, who was residing just up river at the time, in Rock Castle and was built locally by Sean Kingston of Kilmacsimon Boatyard in the old Warehouse at the quay-side (apartments now stand in its place). In 2000, "Naomh Brendan", designed by Rob Jacob, was built by Ray O'Callahan in Kinsale. "Quay Breeze" is the most recent acquisition of the club. It was again designed by Rob Jacob and built by Roddy O'Connor in Midleton. Unlike the previous boats, which were made from timber, this is made from fibreglass and the design of this boat is identical, except in colour, to all other boats used in the All-Ireland Coastal Rowing Championship. As the number of boats increased some of the older boats were sold on to other clubs. "Rock Castle Pride" is now with Myross Rowing Club, and "The May Queen" is with Kilmacabea Rowing Club.

As well as swimming and rowing, the club has expanded itself to become a focal part of the local community. Every year a Christmas Day Swim is organised at Garrylucus strand in Garretstown, with the proceeds being donated to local charities in the area. This event receives great support from the surrounding community, as well as the club members themselves. In addition a Senior Citizens' Party is organised annually at Keohane's Bar in Kilmacsimon.

Like all other community organizations, a large amount of annual funding is required for its successful operation. Sponsorship comprises a large proportion of this and, if it was not for the generosity and support given to the club over the course of its history, it would have been impossible to stay competing year after year at the highest level. Neilus and Sylvia Keohane of Kilmacsimon Bar, John and Kitty O' Leary of O' Leary's Plant Hire, John and Mary O' Neill of Ballinadee Engineering Ltd., Martin Harte of Harte's Well Drilling and Bill and Therese Kelleher of Kelleher's Builders Providers, have been the club's main sponsors down through the years. Schering-Plough (Brinny) Co. has also been a continual supporter of the club. A great debt of gratitude is owed to these people from all those who have benefited and enjoyed being involved with Kilmacsimon Swimming & Rowing Club.

Kilmacsimon Swimming & Rowing Club have always been blessed with great leadership from both the founder members as well as the newer members who have come forward to take up the mantle. This has ensured continuous support and assistance from the surrounding community as well as past and present club members. The recent donation of a site to the club, by Neilus and Sylvia Keohane of Kilmacsimon Bar, means that the club will have its own base for the first time. This has led to great excitement in the area and plans are currently being drawn up for a Clubhouse.

Myross Rowing Club

A six oar gig was commissioned in 1924, confirming that the sport of rowing can be traced back to that date. However, it is believed that boat racing took place prior to 1924 by means of the four oar yawls in use by fishermen at that time.

Rowing has always had a special place in the hearts of the people of Myross Parish. The men who brought pride and honour to their native village are fondly remembered. Indeed the feats of crews and individuals have become part of local folklore.

Vests, worn by the team of 1925 are encased in glass and proudly displayed amongst present day medals and trophies in the Myross Rowing Club Boathouse which was completed in 1999. The panel of oarsmen who crewed the boat in the period 1924 – 35 were men of exceptional talent and stature.

The new six oar gig that was commissioned in 1935 was named after the Patron of the Parish, "St Brigid".

Another great crew came to the fore during the late 1940's who were to match if not surpass their illustrious predecessors.

In the 1950's, we have a tale of much renown, named aptly The Rowing Challenge of 1953, which provides us with an insight into the determination and willingness of previous Myross rowers.

The Rowing Challenge of 1953

In *The Southern Star* of 17th September, 1953, the following notice appeared: "We, the crew of the 4-Oared Glandore Gig, that rowed in the 4 oared gig race in Castletownshend on 9th September 1953, hereby challenge the same Myross crew that rowed in that race to row a further race within the next fortnight at Union Hall Harbour for a stake of £20 on upwards. Acceptance of this challenge to be notified in next week's Star." The notice was signed by Donal O'Donovan, W Farrar, P J Hegarty and M Minihane.

The reason for the challenge goes back to the Castletownshend Regatta of

9th September 1953, when the Glandore crew refused to accept their defeat at the hands of the Myross Men, claiming that they were cheated out of the race. The Myross Junior six had just pulled and Diarmuid O'Donovan, a member of the crew, having completed his rowing for the day retired to Castletownshend for a good "meal". He had just finished the meal when he was prevailed upon by his good friend Joe Sheehy to take part in the 4 oar race, as a member of that crew was missing. Diarmuid knew that rowing on a full stomach would not be a wise thing, but being a man who never failed to accept a challenge, he bowed to Joe's pleadings. On the outward leg of the race with the Myross boat leading, Diarmuid began to suffer the effects of the full stomach and it was agreed that Joe, who was coxman, and himself would change places after rounding the buoy and this they did. The Glandore boat began to pull up on them as the change was taking place, but due to skilful manoeuvring by the Myross men at this stage, and further on in the race, they managed to stay ahead and went on to win the race. The Glandore crew could not accept that they had been defeated by a crew who had to visit for a while, in order to let men change places, and hence the challenge.

In *The Southern Star* of 24th September 1953, the challenge was answered as follows: "We, the crew of the Myross gig, who beat Glandore by

Myross Jnr Ladies, Sandra Glanton, Mairead Daly, Carmel McCarthy, (cox), Niamh McCarthy and Goretti Hayes, the team who won the SW Championship, County and All Ireland in 2001.

four lengths at Castletownshend Regatta, on 9th September 1953, hereby accept the challenge of the Glandore crew to meet them in a further race, and would do so in any part in the South of Ireland at any time. However, we are accepting this challenge provided that the race is rowed in the same harbour with the same crew on Sunday, 4th October 1953, for the stake of £100".

Glandore accepted the challenge, and this stake continued to rise until it reached a figure of £350. Denis O'Donovan N.T., an inhabitant of Union Hall and Principal of Castlehaven N.S., held the money for the Myross men. Besides this stake, there were also many private betting arrangements and a sum totalling £300 changed hands on the day. There was even a bookmaker present in Castletownshend on the day of the race but he did not fare well due to the fact that all bets were laid before the bid day. October 4th 1953, turned out to be a turbulent day, weather wise, but still the race went on, and the Myross gig beat the Glandore gig by many lengths. The crew on the day, as on September 9th, were Diarmuid O'Donovan, Sean Deasy, John O'Mahony, John Hallihane and Joe Sheehy (cox). It is interesting to note that in 1953 not one of the many boats along the coast succeeded in winning at a home regatta.

The Myross crew, encouraged by their wins over Glandore, decided they would take on a crew from Ahakista, who had never been beaten in any regatta. They asked Mr Good of Rineen, for the loan of a 4 oar yawl, which had come off one of the boats delivering supplies to his mill. Not only did he give them the boat, but he also repaired and painted her for them. The crew trained hard, and they eventually came face to face with Ahakista, at Schull Regatta in 1954. Again the Myross crew went on to win this race, and the crew from Ahakista returned home disappointed, never to put to sea again.

As the 1950's began to fade into history, unfortunately the era of the six oar gig ended. But with the coming of a new dawn, a new style boat was produced in the 1960's which generated its own excitement and local rivalry. The birth of the four oar gig was upon us.

In 1963, the Parish of Myross, commissioned a new breed of boat, this time of fibreglass construction. She saw a great deal of success at regattas around the coast, travelling even as far west as Sneem, Co Kerry, during the summer of 1963.

The Parish was fortunate in the mid-1960's to have two boats, which were distinguished and identified by their colour. The white fibreglass boat, based in Union Hall, was to become known as the "Myross White," and her rival, the wooden hulled brown boat based in Raheen, was to become known as the "Myross Brown."

Despite the demise of the four oar gigs, Myross was fortunate in never being without a racing boat.

Another era dawned with the racing boat "Naomh Brid III", a sleekly refined four oar yawl and Myross Parish and a new generation of oarsmen and oars-women continue the proud tradition.

In the 1990's the Club achieved All-Ireland Club of the Year for four years in succession. In 1996 the Club travelled to Carnlough, Co Antrim, where they won three gold, five silver and four bronze medals. The following year in Valentia, Co Kerry, they raised their success level by winning 10 gold, 2 silver and 3 bronze. In 1998 the tally was 11 gold, 1 silver and 3 bronze. In 1999 the Club once again achieved All-Ireland Club of the year.

The official opening of Myross Rowing Club Boathouse took place in September 1999 and was the successful culmination of many years fundraising. It is a well equipped, beautiful building, in a beautiful setting, and enables training to take place all year round.

Myross Rowing Club successfully achieved the All-Ireland Club of the Day title in Schull in August 2001. The Club had an extremely successful season in 2002 and in July the new one design boat arrived in Myross and was raced in August for the first time at the AIB All-Ireland in Carnlough, Co Antrim. Unfortunately they just missed the AIB All-Ireland Club of the Day, which went to their near neighbours, Castletownshend.

The rowing season of 2003 closed with a great finish, the club winning 4 gold medals at the AIB All Ireland held in Cromane, Co Kerry.

The Club has a long history of successes and whilst some reflect on the "Golden Era in the 1940's and 50's" it is difficult to pinpoint its greatest achievements because there have been so many. One thing is certain, all were supreme in their own time.

For all its success, Myross Rowing Club continues to remember those less fortunate and regularly raise funds for local and national charities. By giving in this manner, crew members feel a great sense of fulfilment in the ability of their strengths to yield benefits for others.

Beware if you are asked "are you going rowing" because there's no room for a paddle around the harbour in these waters. It's all very competitive stuff and whilst your eyes might be drawn to the effortless cleave of the boat through the water, the barking of the cox will assail your hearing.

Yawl racing is a sport for the dedicated, the fit and the hardy. Today Myross Rowing Club present teams ranging from Under 12 to Veteran Men's and Veteran Women's. They have a diligent committee who work cohesively as they continue to raise funds through their Weekly Lotto Draw, to maintain the upkeep of their Boathouse and meet ongoing expenses.

Myross Rowing Club Annual Buffet Dinner is held at the end of each season and is always an enjoyable occasion and a time to reflect on past achievements. But perhaps more importantly a time to look forward to another year of successful rowing.

Myross Rowing Club Regatta Committees over the years

Davy McCarthy	Jim Hourihane	Neilus O'Mahony	Connie Hurley
Willie Crowley	Diarmuid O'Donovan	Pat O'Mahony	Joe Sheehy
Dan Hayes	Robbie Limerick	Willie O'Donovan	Paddy O'Donovan
Brian Crowley	Wally O'Neill	Sammy Burchill	Connie Hurley
Pat Hurley	John O'Donovan	Bernie Jennings	Aidan Jennings
John Coughlan	Paddy Coughlan	Christy Murphy	Maurice McCarthy
Ritchie Browne			

Rising Sun – now Galley Flash.   **Blessing of Galley Flash.**

(1964) John Deasy (Kilbeg), Pat Deasy, Bill Deasy, Donie Deasy (Myross) and Maurice McCarthy, Union Hall.

The new one design yawl arrives at Myross Rowing Club 2002.

Padraig Murphy, Castletownshend & Pat Feen, Rushbrooke.

Kilmacsimon SW Snr Championship Winners 1985, Pat O'Neill, Mick Murphy, Eddie O'Neill, Patrick Morgan and JJ McCarthy.

Galley Pre vet Ladies. South-West Champions and County Winners. Niamh Hayes cox, Elaine Lombard, Claire O'Donovan presenting Donal O'Donovan Memorial County Cup, Bernie O'Donovan, Ellen May Ahern and Lois Hurley.

Union Hall Regatta Day.

Carnlough 2002, Intermediate: 1st Myross, 2nd Galley, 3rd Schull.

Galley Junior Men 1985, Senior Men 1986. Noel Fitzpatrick, cox, Denis Murray, Mike Feen, Donal O'Donovan (RIP) and Jim Fitzpatrick.

**Schull
Regatta Day.**

Kilkern Lake Regatta.

Richie Browne, Chairman of Myross Rowing Club Holds Club of the Day plaque for 3rd Year in a row at Schull 2001.

Galley Flash All Ireland Winners 1998: Seamus O'Donovan, Finbarr McCarthy, Julie Harrington, cox, Micheal Harrington & Kenneth Cullinane.

Myross Intermediate Crew 2003: Sean McCarthy, Rory O'Neill, Damien Collins, cox, Kevin McCarthy and Tim Daly.

Shane Crowley, Ian Hurley, Declan Crowley cox, Jamie O'Driscoll, Damien O'Neill, Castletownshend, 2003.

2003 Vet Ladies Castletownshend, Liz Dennehy, Margaret Cahalane, Shane Crowley, cox, Tess Cahalane, Sarah Gornall.

Longboat competition in Bantry 2003.

The Bantry Longboat competing in 2003 against Wales & N. Ireland in Bantry Bay.

Union Hall Regatta.

Dick Kelly President, Castletownshend Rowing Club, Ina and Pat Deasy, President of SWCYRA, and Fr Charlie Sweeney.

Built in the mid-1960's the Myross gig crewed by the 2002 Ladies' team.

Myross Jnr Ladies 2004, Patricia O'Donoghue, Niamh McCarthy, Mairead Courtney and Aisling O'Neill.

Schull Veteran Ladies, Deirdre Hegarty (stroke), Tina Whelan, Patrick O'Brien (cox), Mary O'Callaghan, Kathleen O'Callaghan, winners Union Hall Regatta, 2003.

Clon Mixed 1980's John Madden, Eileen Quinlan, Gobnait O'Riordan, Betty O'Neill and John Quinlan.

Castletownshend Pre-Vet Men, All Ireland Champions Schull 2001, back from left, Paddy Hurley, Brendan O'Neill, Front from left, cox Shane Crowley, John Hurley and Seamus Walsh.

Courtmac training, in Courtmacsherry Bay, July 2004.

Kelly & Lisa Cahalane, Siobhan Cahalane, Siobhan Courtney & cox Declan Crowley, Castletownshend Rowing Club.

Clon Rowing Club make presentation to Courtmacsherry & Inchydoney Lifeboat July 1991.

Ardfield/Rathbarry at the Giants Causeway, 2002 All Ireland, Carnlough, Co Antrim.

Kilmacabea U16 girls 2003.

Fastnet Flyer III: Schull try out their new one design boat, Easter Sunday 2003.

Teddy Burns proudly holds the 2001 All Ireland Club of the Day Trophy at Schull.

Rosscarbery Regatta July 1998.

Sherkin Regatta – Races underway July 1998.

Galley Flash at Rosscarbery Regatta July 1998: Ann Crowley, Bernie O'Donovan, Seamus O'Donovan, Declan O'Regan, cox James Fitzpatrick.

Kilbeg Beach, Union Hall on Regatta Day.

Kilmacabea Under 12s at Castletownshend Regatta 2002

Bantry & Castletownshend represent Ireland at La Grande Motte, Montpellier, France in the World Coastal Rowing Challenge, October 2004.

Castletownshend Snr Ladies train at Bantry for World Challenge 2004.

First Crew: Pat Joe Harrington, Denny Hayes (RIP), Michael O'Donovan (RIP), Mike Feen, cox John Cullinane.

Glandore 4-oar ladies 1981: Cox Adrian Bendon, Anne Kelleher, Aileen Calnan, Mary Calnan, Dory Street.

Boys from the Galley bought the Rising Sun (Baltimore Boat) from Billy O'Driscoll October 1984: l to r Barry McSweeney (RIP), Pat Joe Harrington, Denny Hayes (RIP), Billy O'Driscoll.

Myross: Brendan O'Neill, Martin Limrick, Patrick Deasy, Patrick O'Mahony Richie Browne.

First Bantry Snr Crew of 1963, John Hunt, Tom Mullins, Jackie McGrath, Matt Murphy and Tom "Ginger" Downey.

Rosscarbery Launch of Boat June 1995.

Ring Rowing Club

In 1985, four local young men, Ger O'Driscoll, Charlie McCarthy, Carl Wycherley and Denis Harrington, realising the potential of Ring Harbour as a water sport amenity, decided to purchase a rowing boat for yawl rowing.

Subsequently it was decided to form a rowing club, as interest in the sport grew very quickly. This new club became known as Ring Rowing Club.

Its first chairman and secretary were, Carl Wycherley and Ger O'Driscoll respectively. The boat which had been purchased from "The Rising Sun Club" in Baltimore was renamed "The June Rose II" in honour of "June Rose I", a famous local pilot boat of the early part of the twentieth century. Success was immediate and the Club chalked up many wins over the next few years.

In that first year of competing, in 1985, the club won "Club of the Year", scoring a total of 589 points out of a possible 945. Pulling off first class honours for the Ring Club that season were their U-12, U-16, Two Oar Men's, Two Oar Ladies, whereas their Senior and Junior Men's, Ladies and Mixed teams all managed to take second place in their respective categories.

In the same year they also tucked four "All-Ireland" titles under their belts. This was a truly outstanding achievement which was credited to Flor Deasy, Jimmy Calnan and Brawney Wycherley, selectors and trainers, who dedicated a great amount of time and effort to the club. In 1988 a new boat was commissioned from Mr Billy O'Driscoll of Baltimore, a renowned builder of boats of this class. The new boat was named "Ring Rose" and differed in construction, being a clinker built boat, whereas "June Rose II" was carvel built.

In 1992, another new boat was commissioned, "An Fainne Nua" which was also carvel built. This boat was built by Mr Ted Geary from Cobh. Unfortunately, success in this boat can only be described as moderate. Even though a number of alterations were made to this boat, it proved to be unsuccessful.

In 1996 another new boat was commissioned, being named as "The Ring Rose II" which was carvel built also. She was built by Ray O'Callaghan from

Pride of Ring U 21 team County Championship Final in Glandore on 30th August 1992, when Ring won the U21 race. Cox, Noel O'Donovan, Stroke, Don Coakley, 2nd Bow, David Jennings, 2nd Stroke, Anthony Harrington, Bow, John Duggan. Passage were second and Cobh Fishermen's were third. Ring won the race by the narrowest of margins. The Passage team had won U12, U14, U16, U18 and U21 championships and never rowed together again as a team after this defeat. Ring had four boats in their club's history. June Rose II, Ring Rose, An Fáinne Nua and the Ring Rose II. The boat in the picture is the Fáinne Nua.

By John Duggan

Kinsale. The boat was launched by Mr Jim O'Keeffe TD on Easter Sunday, April 1996. A large crowd gathered to witness this happy event which made the season ahead look promising. Unfortunately only three teams had success, which were U-18, U-12 and Ladies. Gradually from here on due to emigration, lack of membership in the school leaving age bracket, the strength of the Club was reduced severely. And sadly the Club's participation at Regattas ceased.

However, in 2001, after a long absence, the "Ring Rose II" was relaunched back in the water by one of the Club's original founding members, Mr Ger O'Driscoll.

Interest in the Rowing Club quickly grew and soon the Club were again participating at regattas. As the standard of rowing in the South West is now at its highest ever, it will be difficult for the Club to meet the standard.

However, with the spirit of the large number of youths, and the proud tradition of rowing in the village, it is hoped that once again the Ring Rowing Club will be a formidable force in the future.

Written by Donal Calnan and Margaurite Deasy

Rosscarbery Rowing Club

Rowing in Rosscarbery, dates back to 1935 when the first Carbery boat was built by O'Mahony's of Castletownshend. The first Six Oar Gig race took place in Union Hall on August Monday of 1935. Crew members that day were, Jerry and his brother Jimmy Hayes, Pack and Jim Flavin, Paudie Minihane, Jer Charlie Flavin, and cox was Pat Neil. They also won the Four Oar Gig race that day. The first Four Oar yawl boat was built by Mr Murphy of Bere Island in the mid-60's. There were different races against crews from Glandore, Lisheen and Long Island near Schull.

Rowing lapsed in Rosscarbery until 1987. Since then the club has built three boats, the "Carbery", "Ros Ailithir" and "Cliodhna's Wave". Over the years, skilful training by appointed club members and commitment by crew members has brought great achievements to Rosscarbery Rowing Club.

1996 was one of the first great highlights for the club. Crew members proved themselves by being one of the top three clubs participating in the All Ireland Yawl Rowing Regatta held in Carnlough, Co Antrim. The small rowing club, brought big honour and glory home on 26th August, the night of the Rosscarbery Fair, with four gold, two silver and one bronze medal.

The first gold medal winners, Intermediate Men, Michael Harte, Mike Walsh, Joe Ryan, Kevin O'Neill. U-21, Niall Ronan, John Cahalane, Arthur McNulty, Vincent Harte, U-18 boys, Michael Harte, Conor O'Callaghan, Jerome McCarthy, Denis O'Donovan, U-18 Girls, Ane Marie Flavin, Liz Smith, Emma Shanahan, Haley Milthorpe, cox Catherine Hicks.

Silver medal winners were, Junior men, P Ryan, Conor O'Callaghan, Jerome McCarthy, Denis O'Donovan, U-16 Ladies, Rachel McCarthy, Liz Smith, Haley Milthorpe, Michelle Kiely.

Bronze medal winners were, Junior Ladies, Anne Marie Flavin, Rosemarie Fitzpatrick, Catherine Hickes, Marette Hubbert. Coxes that weekend were Catherine Hicks and Vincent Harte.

In 1999 Rosscarbery Rowing Club again finished in third place overall in Rings End in Dublin.

Launch of boat 1995.

Gold medal winners were, U-14 Boys, Christopher Hayes, Mark O'Callaghan, Colin Crowley, Mark O'Callaghan.

An inspiring U-12 crew came in 2nd place, Cathy Duggan, Adele Jennings, Catriona O'Donovan, Owen O'Mahony.

Also narrowly beaten into 2nd place were the U-14 Girls crew, Claire O'Callaghan, Vicky Jennings, Mairead Duggan, Frances O'Donovan.

Bronze medal winners were, U-21 team, Ml Harte, Jas O'Donovan, John Walsh and Ml O'Mahony.

Bronze medal winners, Jnr Men, Niall Ronan, Vincent Harte, Jas O'Donovan, Conor O'Callaghan.

Gold for the Intermediate, Michael Harte, Alan Ronan, Niall Ronan, Tim Crowley.

Coxes over the weekend were Catherine Hicks, David Jennings, Vincent Harte and Mike Walsh.

The first big event hosted for 2000 was the "Millennium Challenge". This was held on the Easter Weekend as part of the annual Oyster Festival. Twenty teams participated in this two day championship which was held on the Ross Lagoon.

£1,000 worth of cash prizes was divided amongst the winners where Killorglin won, Schull came 2nd and Myross 3rd.

Older rowing members have come and gone on but are rich in memory of the excitement of a great race on a harvest summer's evening. Each year the achievements of the past embrace the future when the springtime bustle of the youth awaken in the Lagoon when the rowing season commences.

And each season comes to a close with the autumn evening barbecue by the lakeside enjoyed by some with songs, by others with intense debate about a race narrowly lost or taken. Inexplicably it's that special thing about rowing that makes it more than just a sport.

Schull Yawl Rowing Club

Schull Regatta has had a long and glorious history, which has been the highlight of the Summer in the area for over a century. In that time, epic battles for victory were fought in many a sailing and rowing race. Strangely enough, even though there was huge local interest in the rowing races and the crowds were fiercely partisan in their allegiances, there was no rowing club in Schull itself.

In the Spring of 1996, it was decided to remedy this deficiency. Thomas Newman and Dave Galvin called a meeting to form a rowing club in Schull. That night Schull Yawl Rowing Club was formed. The meeting was well and enthusiastically attended. Dave Galvin was elected Chairperson, Eleanor O'Driscoll as Treasurer, the late Fred Stolberger as Secretary and Thomas Newman as PRO. In less than a year £14,000 was raised, which was spent on two boats, oars and trailer. "The Fastnet Flyer", which was the first, was bought from Rosscarbery for £600. She was a venerable, clinker-built craft, but stripped and painted, under the guidance of Michael O'Driscoll, and with her name proudly emblazoned on her stern, she was a pretty sight. She was blessed and launched in June 1996 by the late Fr Jerome Hurley and by Canon Hilary Wakeman.

Although she was well loved and bravely rowed, that first "Flyer" was at a disadvantage, racing as she was against newer, lighter, sleeker boats. However, she came third across the line at Baltimore Regatta in the Senior Men's race that year. Rowing were Damien Cogan, John Logan, Danny Logan and Vincent O'Regan with John Joe O'Sullivan at the helm.

In 1997 the Club took delivery of the "Fastnet Flyer II". She was of a similar design to the other boats in the South West, and with the new boat, the club went on to gain success in the South West and at County and All Ireland level. That year also saw the sad and unexpected death of Fred Stolberger. We are lucky to have his wife Anne, as Honorary President of the Club, a role she fills actively and positively.

With the arrival of the "Fastnet Flyer II" a new era of fun on the water had

Fr Nolan, Revd Eithne Lynch, Rabbi Julia Neuberger, Susan Grainger and John McGowan.

Deirdre Hegarty, Tina Whelan, Patrick O'Brien (cox), Mary O'Callaghan & Kathleen O'Callaghan. Vet ladies 2003 winners, Union Hall Regatta.

arrived. With the new yawl, the club went on to win the U18 and Senior Men's All Ireland in Valentia.

In 1998 a new committee was elected with Bernie O'Regan, Treasurer and Patsy Goggin, Secretary. This committee did sterling work for the club, and in 1998 Junior Men and Senior Men won All Ireland titles at Kinsale. The following year Dave Galvin replaced Mary O'Driscoll as chairperson and Bernie O'Regan and Patsy Goggin retained their positions. In 1999 the Snr Men were 2nd in the All Ireland in Dublin.

At the 2000 All Ireland in Wexford the Club took U16 Girls, U18 Girls, Veteran Ladies, Senior Men and Club of the Day. In 2000, the committee consisted of Nick Norris as Chairperson, Eleanor O'Callaghan as Treasurer and Pete Wiggins as Secretary. This committee had a two-year tenure. Under its leadership one of the most successful All Ireland Championships were held in Schull in August 2001. The success of this event was a wonderful achievement by a dedicated and hard working committee.

The committee for 2001–2002 has bid a reluctant but grateful farewell to Nick Norris, whose duties as Chairman of the South West Yawl Rowing Association take up much of his spare time. Following Nick Norris's departure, Pete Wiggins was Chairperson, Bernie Driscoll is Secretary and Mary O'Callaghan is Treasurer. The 2004 committee consist of John McGowan, Chairperson, Vice Chair, Michael Hegarty, Secretary, Deirdre Hegarty, Treasurer, Mary O'Callaghan, PRO, Gene Griffin and Club Captain, Stephen Sloane.

Successes at All Ireland level include:

1996	Valencia	1st U-18 Boys, 1st Senior Men
1998	Kinsale	1st Junior Men, 1st Senior Men
2000	Wexford	1st U-16 girls, U-18 girls, Vet Women, Snr Men, Club of the Day.
2001	Schull	2nd U-14's, Veteran Women, U-18 girls, Pre-Vet Women, Junior Women, U-21 Men, Senior Men. On this occasion we had to be content with seven silver medals, three of them albeit, in races that had a photo finish.

We may not have won gold, or Club of the Day on that glorious weekend, but Schull Yawl Rowing Club was a winner in many ways over these three days. The sense of fun, the joyful co-operation, and the wholehearted support of the entire community, made the All Ireland Coastal Rowing Championships of 2001 a truly memorable event. The All-Ireland 2001 working committee of Schull Rowing Club consisted of Nick Norris, Luke

"Fastnet Flyer 3" launched Easter Sunday 2002.

Delaney, Pete Wiggins, Thomas Newman, Dan Joe Cotter, Mary O'Callaghan, Tom Brosnan, Florence Newman, Kathleen O'Callaghan, Eleanor O'Callaghan, Gene Griffin, Bernie Driscoll, Stephen Sloane, Michael O'Driscoll, John Loan, Damien Cogan, Tania McCollum and Fr Michael Nolan.

Into a new era with the one design yawl.

Schull Yawl Rowing Club's new Carbon Fibre Racing Boat, "Fastnet Flyer 3", was launched on Easter Sunday, 2002, by Susan Grainger, of sponsors Grainger Saw Mills, Enniskeane, following blessings by Fr Nolan, Revd Eithne Lynch and Rabbi Julia Neuberger.

We now look forward to a whole new chapter with a new boat and lots of enthusiasm and energy from a broad based, positive and forward looking membership who have Carnlough 2002 firmly in their sights.

Sherkin Island Rowing Club

Sherkin Island Rowing Club has come a long way since 1977 when four young men, brothers, Vincent and the late Barry O'Driscoll, Jimmy O'Driscoll, from the Island and Paul Dinan from Cork City, borrowed Pat Connie O'Driscoll's fishing yawl and rowed in three regattas. One regatta was in Schull and one in Ballydehob, the venue for the third has been lost in history!

In 1978, the late Barry O'Driscoll bought a rowing boat for £200 which he paid for out of his own pocket. That year there was one change in the rowing team with Anthony O'Reilly replacing Jimmy O'Driscoll and their cox was Patrick Collins, from Baltimore.

In 1979 a new boat was commissioned and built in Baltimore, by Danny K O'Donovan, a shipwright. This boat cost £600, one third of the price paid by the then owners of the Jolly Roger. She was christened the "Jolly Roger". This was the first year that Sherkin had a Ladies' team. They were Patricia and Pauline O'Driscoll, and Dolly O'Reilly, from Sherkin, and Kathleen Sheehy from Baltimore. This was quite a successful team winning a number of races.

At the 1979 Union Hall Regatta, the winning ladies' crew consisted of D McSweeney, cox, P O'Driscoll, D O'Reilly, E Sheehy and P O'Driscoll Winners of the four-oar men's open race at the same regatta were, P Collins, cox, A O'Reilly, P Dineen, B O'Driscoll and A O'Driscoll. In 1987 a new boat was bought from Billy Andy O'Driscoll from Baltimore. She was called the "Rising Sun".

The following year, the "Island Breeze" was built by Raymond O'Regan and Lawrence Harrington, boat shipwrights from Baltimore. She was rowed with some success for a number of years. Brendan Cotter, cox, Cormac O'Driscoll, Stephen Casey, Michael Murphy and Barry Murphy won the senior race at Glandore Regatta in August 1989, in the Island Breeze.

The present boat was built in Kilmacsimon, "Island Breeze 2", and is built to the current standard design of the Rowing Association.

Sherkin Island Regatta July 1998.

Rowing Achievements

As far as our memories can aid us, we believe that the first real success in the club was the winning of the Senior Men's West Cork Championship in 1988.

This team then travelled to Wicklow with a senior women's team also to compete in the first All Ireland Regatta.

Results from that competition were as follows:

Senior Women, 1st

Senior Men, 2nd.

The following year the senior men won the West Cork Championship again. The next recorded success was in 1995 when the Senior Men were pipped by Myross in Glandore in the final race of the season for Myross to take the Championship.

The next year, with the new boat, the club went in search of success in many age groups for one of the first times ever.

The notable achievements that year were a Senior 2nd in the local Championship and a Senior and Intermediate 3rd in the All-Ireland in Carnlough.

The Club then stopped rowing for a couple of years due to lack of numbers, but came back with a bang in 2000 when a number of notable successes were achieved at the Wexford All-Ireland.

Senior Women – 2nd
Junior Women – 3rd
Mixed – 2nd
Intermediate Men's – 2nd.

One notable mention should be that of the late Des Buggy, who passed away in 2002, and who was an integral part of both Sherkin Rowing Club and Regatta. Thank you, Des.

Regattas and Rowing

The history of regattas in Bantry is linked to the story of rowing in West Cork and Kerry.

Whiddy Island

Whiddy Island supplied the rowing crews from the earliest times, to the start of the 1960's. The earlier races used six oar seine boats, and one of the earliest wins recorded was by Whiddy in 1911, the crew of which was made up of three brothers, Peter Downey's father, Jack, and his two uncles, Mickey, and Paddy who acted as cox, James O'Leary (Grandfather to the present O'Leary's of Whiddy), and Denny O'Leary. In this year, 1925, the Whiddy crew went to Killarney and were able to borrow a boat there for the regatta, which event was run in two heats. Whiddy won their heat and then entered the final in a different boat, which they also won. Jack Downey broke his leg in 1926, whilst unloading a coal boat in Bantry, as the horse bolted and a keble struck him, so he rowed no more in competition after this.

The committee boat in those days was the "Mary Audrey", owned by the Holland brothers, Dan, Mick and Paddy of Kealanine. She was originally built for Biggs of Bantry, and used as a fishing boat during the summer months, and for raising sand during the winter. She was taken over by the Free State Government during the Troubles and used for communications along the south coast.

The Whiddy crew, including the three Downey's, Jack, Paddy and Ginger, who was later to become famous as the cox in the first Bantry crew, had a rowing history stretching back to nearly fifty years. Mrs Fitzsimons, whose husband was manager in the Provincial Bank, took the photograph. (See p. 78.) They lived in the Bank House for a period, which was owned by Danny Downey. The Fitzsimons had a two-oar boat, which was rowed by Kitty Fitzsimons and Bessie Warner, and steered by Paddy Downey. They rowed all over West Cork and won almost every race that they entered.

Bill Shanahan, uncle of Tead, was stroke oar, third oar was John Moore and they rowed a blue gig which was built by Denny (Kilderry) Keohane. This gig was brought into Whiddy on a Sunday, not fully complete, and taken to Castletownbere on the Monday, on board the "Ebeneezer" owned by Mick O'Sullivan of Marino Street, where she was taken ashore at Watson's Point. Mick O'Sullivan, who was also a carpenter, carried out the finishing touches and applied the canvas. The Downey's Sand Boat or the Princess Beara, skippered by Danny McCarthy of Scart Road, with stoker, Danny Goggin, would also transport the gig in those days. With the arrival in town of Warner's lorry, transport by road was then possible to the other seaside towns.

The dominant rowing crew at this time, was the Shines from Sneem, who were later to be replaced by the Caseys, again from Sneem, who went on to become renowned in wrestling and boxing. The Caseys won their first race in Glengarriff in 1931, and afterwards held an unbeaten record against Danny and Timmy Minehane, and Sammy and Willy Warner, with Mickey Downey steering.

Bantry 1920's to 1940's

In the late 1920's, Bantry town made an entrance into the arena. The crew commissioned a gig from Kilderry Keohane, and it was most unusual, in that tin was used instead of the usual timber to sheet her. There is no record of any win by this boat or crew.

In the 1920's, the Casey's were superior to all comers, and Whiddy had to wait until the late 1940's, for the arrival of Denis O'Leary, Paddy Goggin, Paddy Daly and John Burke, steered by Mick Leary, to again have a winning crew.

Bantry Regattas

Bantry regatta ceased around this time, caused largely by the Second World War. As there were no Whiddy crews available during the early fifties, the Bere Island crews borrowed their boats, until Mike Fitzgerald built a new gig for Bere Island. Regattas again became popular in the 1950's, and Bantry regatta was once again running in 1957. This regatta was particularly famous because of the race between the older Whiddy crew of Denis O'Leary, Paddy Goggin, Paddy Daly and John Burke, steered by Ginger Downey, against the newcomers of Paddy Driscoll, Jim Leary, Con O'Sullivan and John Minehane, steered by Denis Burke. Because of a northerly gale, the usual triangular course was abandoned in favour of a race straight out from Whiddy Island to Bantry Pier. All the money was on the younger crew of Paddy Driscoll and co, but the veteran crew of Denis O'Leary and co, beat them, which caused a fair bit of controversy at the time.

This Regatta was also renowned for the fact that Big Tom O'Sullivan of Gearhies, came second in the Pig and Pole event, which was a notable feat, as this was regarded as one of the most challenging of events, requiring great skill and courage.

Crowleys of Ardralla

During the early 1950's, the Crowleys of Ardralla arrived on the scene, but at that time they were rowing six oared boats on the south coast. The first gig they rowed, which was built by Mick Fitzgerald, was borrowed from Bere Island. Once they started competing, they immediately became unbeatable. This was to start one of the more interesting phases of rowing, as they were the first crew from the south to be very successful. This caused a huge increase in interest in the sport because, along with the traditional rowing followers, they also attracted the followers of Road Bowling, for which the south coast is famous. Road Bowling, which as anyone who has followed the sport will know, is renowned for the amount of betting money involved.

The above gives the pre-history of the modern regattas as we know them.

Revivals

Bantry regatta was revived in 1957 after a lapse of about twenty years. The principal committee members were Sean Dillon, Paddy Minehane (West End), Frank Donovan, Jerry Callaghan, Con Callaghan, Dan Gallagher, Davie Mahoney, Paddy Hourihane, Paddy Cronin, Joe Monks, Moss Collins, Con Harrington, Brendan O'Keefe, Fergus Williams, Donald Costigan, Chairman, Billy O'Donovan and Dan McCarthy – secretary, Teddy Roe – Treasurer, Albert Venn, Sonny Horgan, Ambrose Maher, Fred Burkett, Jimmy Crowley, Mickey Donoghue and Jim O'Driscoll. A noted sailor at the time, Christy Crowley, was the commentator during events. He was selected because of his very good nautical knowledge, and great eloquence. The committee boat was now provided by Mickey O'Donoghue, owner of the "Joanna Mary", for which reason he sailed over from Schull every year.

The First Revival

The first day of its revival, not surprisingly, opened with a gale from the west, and so conditions were too bad for any event to take place in the outside harbour. It was decided to call a meeting in GW Bigg's offices in The Square to discuss the situation. There was a general feeling of gloom, and the opinion was that the regatta should be cancelled. Mickey O'Donoghue, however, suggested that as high water was at 4 p.m., why not hold it in the inner harbour, east of the pier. This was accepted and it proved to be a great success, to the relief of all concerned, as if the event had been cancelled after such a big lapse of time, it would have been very difficult to get the necessary momentum behind the movement again. It was at this regatta that the famous race between the two Whiddy gigs took place.

At this time other events besides rowing were catered for, such as swimming, which was taken very seriously, sailing, and fun events such as Pig & Pole etc. Pleasure boats were also very popular, with crews from Cork City clubs, Blackrock, St Finbarrs and St Michaels, and also crews from Fermoy and Killarney. As regattas and country agricultural shows were the main sources of entertainment during the summer months in the fifties, they tended to draw very large crowds. The fact that Bantry was served by the rail road, proved to be a huge advantage, as once the regatta became established, its reputation for entertainment, and the excellent skills portrayed by the various crews resulted in huge interest from further and further afield.

Bantry also had the added advantage of being a naval port, resulting in the presence of a vessel from the various Irish and European countries for each regatta, adding to the lively atmosphere.

The second year, which was particularly fine, had a British destroyer present in the Bay. The crew were invited to come up with something to add to the entertainment. They put a number of launches in the water in front of the bathing box, and staged a mock battle, with boarding parties, ramming and attempted sinking of the vessels. This proved to be one of the best events of the regatta.

The barbecue and dance, which was held in Bantry House, was to bring the final touches to the growing glory of the festival, as when success led to success, it was turned into a five-day event. The music was supplied by the Regal, the premier dance band in Ireland at the time. A huge bonfire was lit and the fun began. As big as the area was, at times people had to be refused entry. The atmosphere on a fine August evening was absolutely fantastic, and lasted long into the night, with the music echoing out over Bantry Bay.

Regatta Day 1959

The regatta, the following year, Sunday 9th August 1959, was again held in fine conditions. It was, by now, one of the biggest events in West Cork. The train that morning from the city, had standing room only, and had to return to Dunmanway to collect those left behind. The Baltimore branch train was similarly packed. Wolfe Tone Square had walking room only, and from the Old Courthouse to the Abbey, was almost impassable to traffic. There were a large number of pubs in town, and as the day wore on, it was impossible to gain entry to any one of these.

The presence of bookies in the Abbey Road brought the excitement of the races to the event, as at this stage, Ardralla were attracting huge numbers of the betting fraternity. The bookies arrived early in the morning, in order to claim their spot, and erect their chalkboards. As the afternoon wore on, the tic tac started, and the odds were lengthened or shortened as the final event approached. This, of course, was the senior gig race, which usually took place at 5.30 p.m. but more usually at 6.30 p.m. Ardralla were normally the favourites, but huge amounts of money would be placed on the number of lengths they would win by, or who might come second or third. It was becoming a very serious business.

The regatta committees provided the organisation, money, hard work and most of all, the volunteers to stage the events, which took many long hours and numerous meetings over the winter months to plan.

The committees also provided a boat for starting the races, but once the

The first Bantry Senior crew of 1963, John Hunt, Tom Mullins, Jackie McGath, Matt Murphy and Tim "Ginger" Downey.

race started, the competitors were a long way off from the committee boat. It was therefore hard to enforce rules and regulations. Sometimes a committee might be slightly indifferent about same, owing to the large sums of money at stake. Other pressures were inclined to take over.

Bantry Rowing Begins

In 1962, Tom Mullins was at the Bantry Regatta watching the various events, with Ardralla winning as usual. He wondered at the lack of a Whiddy or Bantry crew in the gig races. At this time Whiddy had no one of rowing age. He decided to make an attempt over the winter and spring to get a crew organised for the following season. Receiving full co-operation from the people of Whiddy, he requested a loan of their gig. The only conditions made, were, that the gig would be returned in good condition, and that an experienced Whiddy man would cox it. The gig was collected from Whiddy by John Hunt and Matt Murphy, and steered by Buddy Hazel, out to Bantry pier. The new crew consisted of, Ginger Downey, cox, John Hunt, stroke, Tom Mullins, third, Jackie McGarth, second, Matt Murphy, bow. They went aboard at Bantry Pier to commence what was to be an eventful few years. The training commenced on June 6th 1963.

The gig was stored in McGarth's at Gurteenroe. Every evening it was rowed up to Whiddy to collect Ginger, rowed in practice then, for approximately one hour, then back to the bank in Whiddy to drop Ginger, and all ashore to have a chat with the Islanders and pick up some tips from some of the most experienced oarsmen in the south of Ireland. It was then back to McGarth's to store the gig, all of which took at least two hours, six nights per week.

The strenuous training continued until the following August Monday, when the gig was taken to the Castletownbere Regatta, on a lorry owned by Cronin's of Ballylickey. The lorry was packed with supporters of all ages and to carry the surplus numbers, Willie David O'Sullivan hired Barry's bus. The spin on the lorry was one of the highlights of the whole season. The inside floor would be packed, and as many as possible up on the crates to view the creac. Travelling through the various towns, was especially delightful, as if there happened to be any festival or show taking place, the flags across the street were collected to decorate the lorry.

The plan in Castletownbere, was to row the junior race in the regatta and see how they fared, as Ardralla were rowing in the senior event, and nobody in their sane senses would attempt to row against them in their first outing. The course in Castletownbere was usually one of the longest in the circuit, starting inside, out through the perch, around a buoy, then head for Bere Island around the next buoy and back for the harbour. Bantry won this first race handsomely and so were very satisfied with their first outing.

The team returned home for more training and to plan strategy. Many long evenings on Whiddy were spent discussing the pros and cons of going senior in the event in Bantry on the following Sunday. The decision was made to once again row in the junior race, and assess their ability and their chances against Ardralla. The junior race was scheduled for 4.30 p.m. and the senior at 5.30 p.m. The course was a straight run in from Cushroe to the finish, between the committee boat and the bathing box. This was a fairly short course, and was considered to suit Ardralla as they were always away like lightning from the start.

The junior race started, as was usual about 5.15 p.m. This delay in time was always one of the greatest complaints by both participants and audience about regattas, but was something over which committees, to a large extent, had no great control, as anybody who has been involved in the organisation will know. Bantry won again with no great effort, so now the big decision had to be made – row in the senior race after only a short hour's rest, and risk losing both the race and their confidence in themselves, or wait for next year. They also had to take the opinion of their backers into account, who were now willing to chance their money on a fairly untried crew. The decision was made to go for it, and they entered their name for the senior race against Ardralla; and so history was made.

For the first time in their rowing careers, Ardralla were beaten by three lengths. They made a flying start as usual and were gone from the other five boats after about two minutes. This was the leading boat's usual tactic and once clear, they then eased off, rowed handy until the nearest boat came up, then a spurt again and away clear until the next challenge. The hard training Bantry had been doing over the summer months, paid off. However, Ardralla caught up with them about three quarters of the way down the course. Ardralla put on their best effort but it was equalled by Bantry, who then forged ahead, kept the momentum going and finished three lengths clear. There was consternation in West Cork.

Then the debate started. The southern backers had lost a fortune, as they considered these easy pickings. Their pride was hurt, and explanations came thick and heavy; they were caught on the hop; it was a short course; they weren't really fit; and whatever about anything else, they would be ready for the next encounter.

The last one, was the really telling one for Bantry, as even though there was jubilation in the camp, there was a lot of experience in the advisers. There were a few evenings spent in Whiddy, after the training sessions during the week, as there used to be as much learned on the land as on the water. Schull was the next event where the two adversaries would meet again, if Bantry decided to go. Challenges were being issued, limitless money offered, and private contests arranged if necessary.

Bantry opted for Kenmare Regatta instead, succeeded and finished the year as winners. One did not often get the chance to beat Ardralla and the general mood was that it would be nice to keep that feeling for as long as possible. So ended the first season, and the gig and cox were returned to Whiddy intact.

£150 for a New Gig

As the Whiddy gig was at this stage, ready for retirement, it was decided to approach Denny Kilderrey, to start construction over the coming winter. Bantry was fortunate in having one of the best boat builders in Ireland in their own backyard, and there was no doubt that he had very few to match him. His father, Jer, had trained him, but as each was a genius, and so inclined to disagree at times, they decided to go their separate ways, and Denny went to America, where he further increased his experience by building aeroplanes. He said that as part of the interview for the job, the applicants had to make a set of their own tools, which had to be of top quality for this specialised work. A deal to make the new gig was struck at a price of £150. As usual a lot of work went into the collecting of the money, because a large amount had to be paid down, before work would commence. As much time went into the selection of the timber, as only the finest and cleanest of timber could be used.

The keel was laid in April and work went reasonably well, but as Denny was the kind of person who used to like to take a long weekend off occasionally, there would be a few interruptions. But, as he said himself, as the gig was forty feet long, if he only had to go around the bench on the opposite side for a nail, it would all take time. As he had a great head for figures, he sat down one day and calculated that, from start in the morning, to finish in the evening, he would have walked a comparable distance from Ballylickey to Gougane and back again.

Training started in June 1964, with the Whiddy gig. The new brown gig was launched in July at Ballylickey. There was a large crowd present for the event, including Danny Minehane of Whiddy and his son John, who was six years old at the time. He still remembers Denny Keohane sprinkling the boat with Holy Water, with the words to the assembled crew, "My troubles are over now and yours are only beginning." Paddy Driscoll towed her into Whiddy.

A Second Crew

This was also an historic year as now a second crew started up in Bantry.

Whiddy again provided the cox, in the person of Paddy Goggin. This crew was Des Hourihane, Paddy and Denis McGrath (brothers of Jacky), and myself. We were granted the use of the Whiddy Gig, which at this stage was giving problems, especially in the rowlocks. The week before Castletownbere Regatta, we asked a huge favour of the senior crew; could we use the new gig in the junior race. They were understandably reluctant to share. We eventually prevailed, however, and were greatly honoured to be allowed row in her for her first race. Castletownbere was the usual long twenty-minute triangular course and we were fit enough for it, rowed the race and duly won it. Denny Keohane was, of course, ecstatic and so struck off to celebrate. Our misfortunate was just about to start, as when the race was over, as was traditional, we decided to give her a spurt to celebrate our victory. Unfortunately, we were careless about our direction and with boats of all sorts moving in every direction, suddenly there was a massive thud from forward. The boat stopped dead, and we were convinced that she was split asunder, and expected to see water pouring into her at any moment. We looked ahead and could see a gaping hole in the side of a rowing boat, which had crossed our bows unnoticed. We were reluctant to go ashore but we had no choice other than to go in and face the music, with all the warnings we had been given to "mind the gig" now ringing in our ears. We rowed alongside the pier, and to put it mildly, there was a bit of criticism. We expected the worst and got out to examine the damage. There were doubts from all sides as to whether she would be safe to go out on the water again, as after the very heavy collision, there might be hidden damage. Denny Keohane was sent for and was eventually found, surprisingly enough in a public house! He sauntered down the slipway and threw his eye along her. He then put his hand on her nose and gave her a good shake. There was dead silence all around until he stood up and said, "She's perfect, no problem." There was a collective sigh of relief all round and we were released.

The Day Civil War Broke Out

The thoughts of everyone now turned to the serious business ahead. This was now the first opportunity where money and pride, lost the year before by Ardralla in Bantry, could be regained. The senior race was scheduled for 5.30 p.m., as was the usual time in any regatta. Tension was high as the various crews were making their final preparations, greasing boats, putting final whippings on oars and checking foot staffs. The boats were put in the water about thirty minutes before the official race time, in order to give the crews time to warm up and view the course. As was usual in every regatta, nobody expected the race to start on time at any rate. The Bantry crew struck off towards the Perch Rock to loosen out and test the equipment.

With still twenty minutes to go before the official time, looking back towards the starting line, they became suspicious when no other boat seemed to be doing a workout. They decided to head back to be on the safe side and stay with the main group. They were a very wise crew, but were, however, of a very trusting nature. When still about a thousand yards from the starting line, they heard the sound of the shotgun ordering the start. The five boats were coming towards them at full speed. Bantry had to decide whether to turn and go with them or go back to the line and so start officially as it were. They chose the latter and proceeded through the oncoming fleet. Eventually, they turned around and chased after the others to try and join the race. There was pandemonium up town when the word flew around that the senior race had started, as everyone expected the usual forty to fifty minutes delay and were relaxing over a few pints, before strolling down to the beach to view the spectacle. There was a stampede down to the pier to see what happened. They could see the boats disappearing in the distance, with Bantry trailing a long way behind. Castletownbere being such a long course, there was plenty of time for enquiries. The regatta committee was out on the starting boat, and nobody could get to them, which was probably fortunate. After about fifteen minutes, suddenly a shout went up that the first boat could be seen returning. The binoculars were put up and the statement made, "Bantry is ahead". Nobody could believe it. Bantry passed the line about five lengths clear of the pack, and hands were put out to collect winnings, but then no shot was fired for them, and this put a halt to proceedings. Everyone waited for the second boat to cross, and then the gun went up and fired the shot. An announcement was made over the loudspeakers, "Bantry disqualified for being late at the start." Civil war broke out!

An eminent doctor tried to reason with the regatta chairman, and used forceful argument, but to no avail. Billy Shannon, who had been in one of the most distant pubs, arrived on the pier to view the race. When informed that it was all over, and of the results, he proceeded to clear the pier of all spectators, he was so upset. And so ended the Castletownbere regatta 1964.

Next race Bantry. Straight course, fine day, Ardralla using Kenmare Gig, with Brian O'Brien, cox, ahead at the start as usual and led until halfway. Bantry put on a spurt, passed and finished three lengths ahead. All the money lost again, and even more sting in the proceedings. At this stage there were nearly more bookies than spectators along the Abbey Road. Schull awaited, and home country for the challengers. A cold day. Usually a long course in Schull, start inside at the committee boat, then out to a separate buoy for each boat to go around and back to finish at the committee boat. Tactics came into play here. Bantry were afraid of a repeat of Castletownbere and so stayed in their boat close to the start line. As was usual the race was forty-five minutes late starting. When Bantry got fed up with waiting, they would head for the shore where Ardralla were carrying out adjustments. When Bantry came close, Ardralla would put in the water, pull a hundred yards or so, and then return to shore. This happened four or five times with the result that Bantry finished up cold and wet. Bantry were slight favourites, but failed to win, which was a big surprise to their supporters.

1965

In 1965, there were some changes. Tom Mullins and Ginger Downey decided to call it a day. Paddy Goggin was in as cox and I was on the third oar. We started our training again in June, following the same format. Our first outing was Kenmare, which we lost. This was two in a row and there was a lot of murmuring amongst the backers, so the next outing was very important. This was in Castletownshend. I remember saying to John Hunt, "What about Ardralla?" He replied, "Don't mind them, it's the Deasys are going to cause us problems." A long course again, out around a buoy and back in. His words were prophetic. We started off well, and soon there were only two boats in the race. We were first to the buoy, with the Deasys almost with us. It was neck and neck. We were only half a length ahead and could not get clear of them until the very end of the course, when we finished about two lengths ahead. First victory – confidence returning fast.

Next up was Castletownbere, a hard race, but resulting in a win again. Bantry Regatta, home ground, but the wind had been blowing hard the previous day, and was still about force five on the day. This always caused problems crossing the beaches, as a short high sea would build up. We started off well again, but Ardralla were back on form. They were half a length ahead when we started to surf down a steep wave. Our bow nose-dived into the wave ahead and we heeled over and shipped a lot of water. We straightened up with water sloshing everywhere and had lost about two lengths. We had no choice only to press on and when we got into the calm water, we picked up speed again and caught up with Ardralla. They started to cross our bow to cut us off, but Mickey Donoghue was on a catamaran, which was in the Bay for surveying, that could do about 15 knots and he pulled up behind them, and told them to hold their own course or else. We passed them and won by three lengths!

Back to Schull again and their home ground. Their backers had lost a fortune at this stage, as they were not people to do things by half measures, so the pressure was on them, as Schull was usually the last important race of the year. A fine day again. We were reasonably confident for this race – more experienced and well on our guard. We were as good on tactics now as themselves. After a good row on the water early in the day, we came ashore, put on our gear and stayed warm. The usual delays occurred. They put their boat in the water, came back, and carried out minor modifications, then back on the water again. If they started to head towards the starting line, we would embark also and keep in touch. We were on a foreign coast so to speak and had to put up with the local situation. This tit for tat went on for an hour or so. Schull was packed for the occasion and most of the towns in West Cork were deserted, as this was seen as the final, as it were.

Eventually, the backers could see no advantage going to the home side, so the boats were called to the starting line. We all had our own buoy to start from, which the cox held on to, until the shot was fired. We were on the north of the line with, Ardralla four lanes south. The shot went and we were off. As usual Ardralla were gone clear almost immediately. We stuck to dogged rowing with no sprints and eventually started to close the gap. It was a case of attrition. When we came close they would spurt again, but they could not keep it up and we caught them just before the turn. We were quietly confident we could finish the turn and head straight for home. However, it was not to be so easy. Instead of completing their turn around the buoy, they came straight across and cut in front of us. We were then rowing side by side. The course for home would have been straight east, instead we were rowing north-east, towards the land in order to get around them. As we kept going to the left to get around them, they kept coming to the left to block us. If we slowed down to fall behind them, they slowed down as well. At this stage, Johnny Hunt and Jackie McGrath had their oars in the Ardralla gig and their oars in ours. Matt Murphy and myself were rowing clear. It was more like a wrestling match than a rowing race and eventually when seaweed appeared, we knew we were in serious trouble. The rocks were above us and the people shouting right over our heads. Paddy Goggin shouted to stop rowing as we were going aground. So stop we did, with our nose up on a ledge. We backed water to get her out and looked around to se the opposition taking off, clear and away. We were knackered after the efforts and reckoned we were finished as there was so little of the race left. We had a discussion and decided we might as well make the effort anyway, and so took off after them. We thought it was a hopeless task, but driven on by Paddy Goggin, we got on to full speed again. He said we were catching them and looking around we could see the gap closing. Paddy said to go south of them as there was no land there where they could block us. We started to do a large circle south of them, but they came straight across us again. Paddy said we had no choice only to fall in on them. We were oar for oar again, but Paddy had more room this time to keep just the right distance from them. Matt and myself had our oars in their boat, and were able to catch their oarlocks with the blade of the oar so had something to pull against. They then came closer to us to prevent us from rowing at all, so we put our oars against their backs and pulled against them. We were inching ahead all the time, but the finish line was coming closer, and if we finished up on the wrong side of the committee boat, we would be disqualified, so we had to get clear quickly. The struggle continued. Matt and myself got the blade of our oars against the back of their bowman, and second oar and pulled. His next stroke was against the wave breaker, next against the bow and we knew we had them, out clear, turned up for the line and won by four lengths.

If we hadn't won that day, who would have known what would have happened. A fair loss would be no problem, but feelings were so high and there was so much money involved on both sides, what would have been seen as an unfair defeat, could have led to serious difficulties.

During our time rowing together, we had two serious arguments. The first was in Castletownbere when we were leading a race by about twenty lengths. An argument started as to whether we should win by more, or save face for the other contenders by taking it easy. It got so heated that we stopped rowing to discuss the situation. During this madness, Brendan Murphy of Bere Island came over in his launch to enquire if we needed help, as he thought we had damaged some equipment. He was told to bugger off and mind his own business. After a minute or so of discussion we had a vote and decided to continue the race, winning by a fair margin.

At the end of the 1966 season, Bantry receive a challenge to row against the pick of the combined crews at Union Hall Regatta, which we duly accepted. The shot was fired and, after only twenty lengths, the combined crew broke a rowlock. Argument again as to whether we should carry on and take the race as we were entitled to. Vote again to return to start as we wanted a decision as well. The race was restarted and we won by four lengths.

I may have omitted to mention earlier, about the rules and regulations. Strictly speaking they were of the highest standard, were adhered to, and admired by all the people involved, both crews and committees. The only problem was, that once the crews were out of sight of the committee boat (and sometimes not), it was a case of – may the best man win. An example of this was in Glandore Regatta in 1967. This event was usually held on a Thursday evening after Schull Regatta, so that they could benefit from the yachts returning back to Cork. We did not expect any great opposition there, but always supported it, because it is a place of great natural beauty and there would be a dance after the race. It was the usual situation, each boat with its own starting buoy, out its own lane, around a separate buoy and back to the finish. We went out the course to have the usual loosen up and check that all was in order. When we came back in, the two other competitors in the forthcoming race approached us. They informed us that they would not take part in the race unless we agreed to split the prize money. We had no choice but to agree to this proposal, suspecting nothing untoward, as the deal had been made. The race was started and away we go. We had about ten lengths lead after seven minutes, when suddenly we passed two buoys in line, where there should have been three. Paddy Goggin said he could see a third one, about eight hundred yards ahead and this must be ours. It was the usual catch twenty-two. If we failed to carry on and go around it, we would be disqualified, and if we did, we would probably lose the race. Again we held a meeting, vote taken and decision made to press on. Up to this it had been a stroll, but now we had to gallop, up to full speed and head for the buoy. Eventually we rounded our own, and back after them. Lucky for us the course was long enough for us to catch up to them and beat them by about three lengths. Of course the other catch was, that if we lost we would have returned home empty handed.

This year was notable also, in that Bantry for the first time, had a second senior crew – Sandy Gibbons, William O'Brien, Christy O'Sullivan, Joe MacCarthy and Sean O'Mahony, coxed by John Burke of Whiddy and occasionally by James Mahoney. They rowed in a few junior races and did very well before turning senior.

One of our races was against the Deasy's in Castletownbere. At this stage they were starting to come out on top and we were only able to hold our own against them. The usual long race, and we were half a length behind them to the first buoy. They started to round and as they were broadside across us, Paddy Goggin asked us for a sprint. We obliged and next thing we hit them in the very centre of their gig. We then pushed them like a tug, until we had clear water, backed off, rounded inside and cleared for home. The following Sunday, they got their revenge by beating us in Bantry.

That was our last year together. We rowed in many other races and venues, but these were the most interesting ones. The next generation of rowers took over and they are well able to tell their own story.

By Alex O'Donovan
President
Bantry Rowing Club 2004

South West Coast Yawl Rowing Association Committees 1978 to 1989

	1978	**1979**
Chair	Denis Calnan	Denis Calnan
Vice-Chair	Billy O'Driscoll	Billy O'Driscoll
Secretary	Margaret O'Reilly	Margaret O'Reilly
Treasurer	Kieran Cotter	Kieran Cotter
PRO	Don Donoghue	Don Donoghue

	1980	**1981**
President	Denis Calnan	
Chair	Billy O'Driscoll	Denis Calnan
Vice-Chair	Pat McCarthy	Billy O'Driscoll
Secretary	Margaret O'Reilly	Margaret O'Reilly
Treasurer	Kieran Cotter	Kieran Cotter
PRO	Don Donoghue	Don Donoghue
Ctte		Donie Sheehy
		Pauline O'Driscoll
		Pat McCarthy

	1982	**1983**
President	Denis Calnan	Denis Calnan
Chair	Billy O'Driscoll	John Keohane
Vice-Chair	Pat McCarthy	
Secretary	Tom Hayes	Tom Hayes
Treasurer	Billy O'Driscoll	Billy O'Driscoll
PRO	Don Donoghue	

	1984	**1985**
President	Denis Calnan	Billy O'Driscoll
Chair	Finbarr Hegarty	Finbarr Hegarty
Vice-Chair	–	Carol Wycherley
Secretary	Pat Hayes	Mary Hayes
Asst Sec	Mary Hayes	Charlie McCarthy (RIP)
Treasurer	JJ McCarthy	JJ McCarthy
PRO	Denis Coakley	Liam Sheehan

	1986	**1987**
President	Denis Calnan	
Chair	Carol Wycherley	John Keohane
Vice-Chair	John Keohane	Carol Wycherley
Secretary	Mary Hayes	Mary Hayes
Asst Sec	Charlie McCarthy (RIP)	Charlie McCarthy (RIP)
Treasurer	JJ McCarthy	JJ McCarthy
PRO	Liam Sheehan	

	1988	**1989**
President		Pat Deasy
Chair	John Keohane	John Keohane
Vice-Chair		Carol Wycherley
Secretary	Mary Hayes	Mary Hayes
Asst Sec		Denis Coakley
Treasurer	JJ McCarthy	JJ McCarthy
Asst Treas		PJ Harrington
PRO		Liam Sheehan

South West Coast Yawl Rowing Association Committees 1990 to 1997

	1990	**1991**
President	Pat Deasy	Pat Deasy
Chair	John Keohane	John Keohane
Vice-Chair		Carol Wycherley
Secretary	Mary Hayes	Mary Hayes
Asst Sec		Caroline Vickery
Treasurer	JJ McCarthy	JJ McCarthy
Asst Treas		PJ Harrington
PRO		John Hennessy
Asst PRO		Gobnait O'Riordan

	1992	**1993**
President	Pat Deasy	Pat Deasy
Chair	Pat Joe Harrington	Pat Joe Harrington
Vice-Chair	Denis Murphy	Denis Murphy
Secretary	Mary Hayes	Helen McCarthy
Asst Sec	Helen McCarthy	Therese McCarthy
Treasurer	JJ McCarthy	JJ McCarthy
Asst Treas	Eileen Quinlan	Noel Calnan
PRO	Martin McCarthy	Barry McSweeney

	1994	**1995**
President	Pat Deasy	Pat Deasy
Chair	Sean O'Farrell	Sean O'Farrell
Vice-Chair	Denis Murphy	Eugene McCarthy
Secretary	Claire Harrington	Claire Harrington
Asst Sec	Eileen Quinlan	Mary Kiely
Treasurer	Pat Joe Harrington	Pat Joe Harrington
Asst Treas	Colin Bateman	Anthony Harrington
PRO	Barry McSweeney	Con Hurley

	1996	**1997**
President	Pat Deasy	Pat Deasy
Chair	Sean O'Farrell	Bill Deasy
Vice-Chair	Bill Deasy	Eugene McCarthy
Secretary	Con Hurley	Claire O'Mahoney
Asst Sec	Claire Harrington	Anthony Glanton
Treasurer	John Duggan	John Duggan
Asst Treas	Richie Browne	Richie Browne
PRO	Bernie O'Donovan	JJ McCarthy
Scorekeeper	Claire Harrington	JJ McCarthy
Starters	Sean O'Farrell	PJ Harrington
	Den Murphy	Den Murphy
Scrutineers	Richie Browne	Donie Harrington
	Martin McCarthy	Richie Browne

South West Coast Yawl Rowing Association Committees 1998 to 2001

	1998	1999
President	Pat Deasy	Pat Deasy
Chair	Bill Deasy	Bill Deasy
Vice-Chair	Eugene McCarthy	Eugene McCarthy
Secretary	Bernie O'Donovan	Bernie O'Donovan
Asst Sec	Anthony Glanton	Anthony Glanton
Treasurer	John Duggan	John Duggan
Asst Treas	Richie Browne	Richie Browne
PRO	JJ McCarthy	JJ McCarthy
Asst PRO	–	Mike Walsh
Scorekeeper	–	Ann Crowley
Starters	Pat Joe Harrington	PJ Harrington
	Den Murphy	Den Murphy
Scrutineers	Richie Browne	Joe Hawkins
	Donie Harrington	Nick Norris
Camera	–	Joe Hawkins
Ass.	Alan Warner	Bill Deasy
Delegates	Bill Deasy	Eugene McCarthy
	Eugene McCarthy	

	2000	2001
President	Pat Deasy	Pat Deasy
Chair	Bill Deasy	Nick Norris
Vice-Chair	Nick Norris	Richie Browne
Secretary	Carmel Mulcahy	Carmel Mulcahy
Asst Sec	Anthony Glanton	Vincent Harte
Treasurer	John Duggan	Ann Hawkins
Asst Treas	Conor O'Callaghan	John Duggan
PRO	Mike Walsh	Finbarr McCarthy
Asst PRO	Joe Hawkins	John Harrington
	John Harrington	Michael O'Mahony
Scorekeeper	Ann Crowley	Ann Crowley
	–	Eleanor O'Callaghan
Starters	Pat Joe Harrington	PJ Harrington

	Den Murphy	Den Murphy
	JJ McCarthy	JJ McCarthy
Scrutineers	Nick Norris	Dick Kelly
	Richie Browne	Pat McCarthy
Camera	Joe Hawkins	Joe Hawkins
Ass. Camera	–	Conor O'Callaghan
Ass.	Mike Walsh	
Delegates	Niall Ronan	
	John Duggan	

South West Coast Yawl Rowing Association Committees 2002 to 2004

	2002	**2003**
President	Pat Deasy	Pat Deasy
Chair	Nick Norris	Nick Norris
Vice-Chair	Richie Browne	Mick Murphy
Secretary	Carmel Mulcahy	Bernie O'Donovan
Asst Sec	Ann Crowley	Anne Cochrane Townsend
Treasurer	Ann Hawkins	Ann Hawkins
Asst Treas	John Duggan	John Duggan
PRO	Julie Harrington	Julie Harrington
Asst PRO	Alec O'Donovan	Mike Walsh
	Bill Deasy	Joe Hawkins
Scorekeeper	Ann Crowley	Mary O'Brien
	Rosarie Glanton	Helen McCarthy
Starters	Pat Joe Harrington	Mick Murphy
	JJ McCarthy	JJ McCarthy
	Joe Hawkins	Joe Hawkins
	Bill Deasy	Bill Deasy
Scrutineers	Dick Kelly	Dick Kelly
	Mike Feen	Stephen Sloane
	John Barrett	Richie Browne
	Pat Deasy	John Barrett
	Stephen Sloane	Colm Cahalane

Camera	Joe Hawkins	Joe Hawkins
Ass. Camera		Conor O'Callaghan
		Michael Harrington

2004

President	Pat Deasy
Chair	Mick Murphy
Vice-Chair	Mike Feen
Secretary	Bernie O'Donovan
Asst Sec	Anne Cochrane Townshend
Treasurer	Ann Hawkins
Asst Treas	John Duggan
PRO	Julie Harrington
	Mike Walsh
Scorekeeper	Helen McCarthy
	Mary O'Brien
Starters	Joe Hawkins
	Bill Deasy
	JJ McCarthy
	Colm Cahalane
Scrutineers	Dick Kelly
	Stephen Sloane
	Richie Browne
	Mike Feen
	Diarmuid O'Sullivan
	JJ McCarthy
	Pat Joe Harrington
Camera	Joe Hawkins
	Michael Harrington

94